STEPHEN TAYLOR

The Great Australian Kids' Almanac

FOREWORD ii	**HEALTH** 49	**SPORT** 103
ABORIGINES 1	**HERALDRY** 51	Youngest Australian Winners • 108
THE ARTS 4	**HISTORY** 52	Skateboard Riding • 110
Children's Books too Good to Miss • 7	Prime Ministers of Australia • 57	Australian Little Athletics Union • 110
Australian Children's Book Award Winners • 8	**IMPORTS** 58	BMX • 111
Independent Music in Australia • 9	**INDUSTRY** 60	Australian BMX Champions • 112
Countdown Award Winners • 16	**INVENTIONS** 64	**TRANSPORT** 113
The National Music Camp Association • 19	**LIFESTYLE** 66	**TUCKER** 118
The Australian Youth Orchestra • 20	Big Things in a Big Country • 68	**VEGETATION** 122
Dance • 20	A List of Big Things • 69	**WAR** 125
Drama • 21	The Australian Youth Hostels Association • 71	**WOMEN** 130
Youth Theatre Groups • 21		**WORDS** 134
BUSHRANGERS 22	**MEDIA** 72	**WORLD BEATERS** 138
CLIMATE 25	**MONEY** 74	
CREATURES 26	**MYSTERIES** 75	
Gestation Periods of Popular Mammals and Pets • 31	**NAMES** 78	
DISASTERS 32	**PEOPLE** 83	
EVENTS 35	**PLACES** 91	
FALLACIES 38	**POLITICS** 96	
FIRSTS 41	**SHAME** 101	
GEOGRAPHY 44		

ILLUSTRATED BY: PATRICK COOK

ANGUS & ROBERTSON PUBLISHERS

Foreword

All of my life I have been fascinated by facts, and sometimes when I find something that I do not know about I will go to ridiculous lengths to fill the gap in my knowledge. This obsession with wanting to know has led over the years to the collection of thousands of odd facts on cards.

In this book I have put together over 1200 fascinating facts about Australia and Australians; not the standard dry sort of thing found in school books but the odd and interesting.

Did you know that Australia had a link with the American Civil War? That the biggest tree ever cut down was an Australian eucalypt? That Charles Dickens's sons settled in Australia? That a future American president was saved by Australian coast watchers? That Rolf Harris was a swimming champion? That the famous yacht *America*, after which the cup is named, finished its life in Australia? Do you care? If you do, then this is the book for you.

My thanks to all of those who contributed to my store of knowledge over the years. Particular thanks to Margaret Smith and Joy MacCuspie for their encouragement and assistance, and to Jill Brown who typed the manuscript.

I also acknowledge with thanks the special contributions from Dr Belle Alderman for *Books too good to miss*; Ann Kern, *Big Things in a Big Country*; Michael Mackie, *Independent Music in Australia*; Jim Shepherd, *BMX and Skateboard Riding*; *The Australian Almanac*, Australian Bureau of Statistics, Australian Youth Hostels Association, Children's Book Council of Australia, Countdown ABC Melbourne, and the National Music Camp Association.

Aborigines

The flat or cylindrical message sticks carried by Aborigines did not actually carry a message, they simply showed the Aboriginal's authority to deliver his message.
The incised design is thought to have been a crude map to show the messenger where to find waterholes.

In some parts of Australia, particularly on the coast and in the Murray Valley, are the mirrnyong heaps or kitchen middens.
These are mounds of ashes, shells and other debris built up by thousands of years of use. Some are over 3 metres (10 feet) high and the area of a small football ground. They are a valuable source of information for anthropologists.

The first Aboriginal mission was set up in 1795 by the Reverend Samuel Marsden. In later periods the various churches set up missions to convert Aborigines to Christianity and feed and clothe them. These days missions are largely Aboriginal communities which determine their own course with indirect help from church societies.

The Aborigines of north-eastern Victoria used to hold feasts in the summer when the bogong moths clustered in the caves and crevices of the mountains. They would singe off the wings and hair of the moths and bake them into cakes which were regarded as delicacies.

Neighbour was the only Aborigine ever to be awarded the Albert Medal for bravery. In 1912 he was arrested for cattle killing with two other Aborigines. While being escorted to Darwin by a Constable Johns the prisoners crossed the flooded Wilton River (N.T.), and Johns was kicked by his horse and fell into the water. Neighbour dived in and rescued him, despite the chains around his neck. He then revived him and rode 100 kilometres (60 miles) to get help. Johns later became the South Australian Commissioner of Police.

The bunyip, a mythological creature from Aboriginal legends, was supposed to emerge at night to devour human

prey. For most of the 19th century colonists and scientists believed that it actually existed.

Tribal Aborigines were expected to become adult at an early age. Girls were initiated as adults at 12 and boys were initiated at 14.

When European settlement began in Australia there were about 300,000 Aborigines divided into about 500 tribes. The tribe was the largest social unit; it had rights to traditional lands and usually comprised about 600 people. Each tribe had its own language and customs and there was no tribal chief or machinery of government.

Tribal Aborigines usually married on the basis of kinship. In most areas it was believed that the best marriage was one between a man and the daughter of his mother's brother. It was common for a man to have two or three wives.

The Aborigines in cooler parts of Australia smothered their skins with a mixture of ochre and fat to protect themselves from the cold. The oily fat of the emu was most highly favoured. In winter they wore a kangaroo-skin coat with the fur on the inside. In summer they wore only strips of possum skin suspended from a belt. The women also wore a girdle of emu feathers and a plaited headband. A valuable item was a possum-skin cloak, because it took so many skins to make one.

Most people think of the Aborigines as purely nomadic people but in some places where food was plentiful they established permanent settlements. For example, in the Western District of Victoria they had permanent dwellings made out of flat stones, which had thatched roofs. These would house up to 12 people.

The Aborigines used the bull roarer to make a sound warning women and children that a sacred ceremony was about to take place, and to keep away from the area. The bull roarer was a flat piece of wood swung around on a cord of some kind, usually made from bark or skin.

The colonial policies of the 1880s towards Aborigines were based on the assumption that the Aborigines were a dying race, and would soon disappear entirely. Colonial charity led to the Aborigines receiving help in the form of medical treatment, blankets and basic foods, to make their last days more comfortable.

It is estimated that in about the year 2000 the Aboriginal population will be 300,000, the same number that it was in 1788 when the First Fleet arrived. Thus it will have taken 212 years to recover from the shock of European settlement.

Although it is true that many Aborigines were killed by white settlers deliberately, the main killer was disease. The isolation of the Australian Aborigines from the people of Europe and their diseases led to their lack of resistance to the diseases when they were introduced to the country by white people. Thousands died from cholera, measles, chicken pox, pneumonia, syphilis, tuberculosis and particularly smallpox. No health facilities were available to them.

In the eastern part of Australia the Aborigines played ball games before the arrival of white settlers. The ball was made out of tightly wound strips of skin in a leather bag. Both throwing and kicking games were played, not unlike netball and soccer. In Queensland they played a hockey-type game with sticks and a stone.

ABORIGINES

The Aborigines refer to the "dreamtime" which is the equivalent to the Christian idea of Creation. It was a period when ancestral spirit-beings created the Aboriginal world including the landscape, plants, animals, people and their laws and customs.

Aborigines did not achieve wage equality until 1965 and citizenship until 1967. Even so, in many outback areas wage equality still does not exist and Aborigines work for wages well below those given to white employees.

The first Aborigine to be given a knighthood is Sir Douglas Nicholls. Sir Douglas was born in New South Wales and was a professional footrunner and V.F.L. footballer for Fitzroy and Victoria. He became a Church of Christ pastor and was active in the Aborigines Advancement League. He was Governor of South Australia from 1976 to 1977 before retiring due to illness.

Infant mortality is much higher in the Northern Territory than anywhere else in Australia due largely to the higher proportion of Aborigines in the population, with their higher infant mortality. Their infant mortality rate of 15.46 per 1000 live births is nearly half as high again as that for Australia as a whole (10.72 per 1000 live births).

Truganini or "Lalla Rookh" who died in 1876 was claimed to be the last Tasmanian Aboriginal but it is doubtful whether this is true. There were many Tasmanian Aborigines who had been driven to the smaller islands around the coast and there are living descendants of these people.

The Aborigines came to Australia from Asia about 30,000 years ago. Their migration drove the existing inhabitants, a completely different racial group, into Tasmania.

Until the successful referendum of May 1967, the Aborigines were not counted as part of the Australian population and were not regarded as citizens.

Charles Perkins was the first Australian Aborigine to obtain a university degree when he received his Bachelor of Arts in 1965 at the University of Sydney. He was born in a shack at Alice Springs and if it had not been for his success as a professional soccer player he would probably never have had the opportunity to obtain a university education.

In western Arnhem Land exist many examples of the style of Aboriginal art described as X-ray art. Paintings on caves, bark sheets, weapons, coffins and grave posts show the internal details of backbone, alimentary canal, heart, liver, gills and the position of the young of all creatures shown, including snakes, lizards, birds, crocodiles, mammals, fish, and very infrequently, humans.

The returning boomerang was used by the Aborigines mainly as a toy, not as a weapon. Weapon boomerangs are longer, heavier and less symmetrical and they do not return. Not all tribes used the boomerang. In northern Australia they were used only as clapsticks in music making.

Whenever the noun Aborigine or the adjective Aboriginal is used to mean the Australian Aborigines rather than native people generally, it should be used with a capital letter to make that distinction.

Captain Cook wrote in 1770, "From what I have seen of the natives of New-Holland, they may appear to some to be the most wretched people upon Earth, but in reality they are far more happier than we Europeans".

The Arts

The large statue of Burke and Wills which now stands in Spring Street, Melbourne near Parliament House, was originally planned for the intersection of Collins and Russell Streets, but public agitation caused the change of location.

The song, now known as "Botany Bay" which begins "Farewell to old England", was not an Australian song. It first appeared as "Farewell to Judges and Juries" in 1820 in England. It was later used as a comic interlude in several London plays of the 1880s, notably in *Little Jack Sheppard*.

Mrs Aeneas Gunn, who wrote *We of the Never Never* in 1908 lived in the "Never Never" for only about 12 months before her husband died, and then returned to civilisation.

The lagerphone is an Australian invention. This musical instrument made from a broomstick with lager caps nailed to it can be rattled and bounced and played with a serrated rattle stick. It is yet to be adopted by the world's major orchestras.

The first feature film made in Australia was *John Vane, Bushranger*, which was completed in 1904.

The tempestuous "Spanish dancer" Lola Montez, who visited Australia in 1853, was really Irish. She was born Marie Delores Eliza Rosanna Gilbert at Limerick in 1818. During her tour of Australia she horse-whipped the editor of a Ballarat (Vic.) newspaper who dared to criticise her performance.

The great Australian comedian "Mo", or Roy Rene (real name Harry van der Sluys) (1892-1954) was born in Adelaide and educated by Dominican nuns. He first appeared on stage at 10 years of age billed as "Little Roy, the Boy Soprano". Only after his voice broke at 15 years of age did he turn to clowning.

Sir Hans Heysen (1877-1968), the great Australian landscape painter, was born in Hamburg, Germany and migrated to Australia with his family at six years of age.

S. T. Gill (1818-1880) whose sketches of the goldfields are still so popular, died a penniless alcoholic. He was born in England, landed in South Australia in 1839, and went to the goldfields in 1852.

THE ARTS

Well-known professional Aussie and entertainer Rolf Harris was born in Perth in 1930. He went to England in 1952 to further his art studies. It was not until he achieved fame as a performer in England that he was recognised as an entertainer in Australia.

Dame Joan Hammond, the great Australian soprano, is really another New Zealander, although she has spent most of her life in Australia.

Australia's oldest surviving feature film is probably *The Story of the Kelly Gang*, made in Melbourne in 1906 by the Tait Brothers. It runs for 67 minutes.

In the early 1940s two Australian poets, James McAuley and Harold Stewart, wrote a series of poems which were deliberately meaningless and made up of unrelated words. They sent them as a hoax to the magazine *Angry Penguins*, using the pen-name Ern Malley. The editors and critics hailed them as works of genius even after the hoax was admitted.

One of the early recording stars on the newfangled gramophone records in 1904 was the South Australian baritone, Peter Dawson. For many years he was the biggest-selling Australian recording star. Re-issues of his records are still sold.

One reason for the excellence of the collection in the National Gallery of Victoria is the purchase of so many exhibits by the Felton Bequest. Alfred Felton was a druggist and general merchant who left nearly £400,000 to art and charity. Half of that went to the National Gallery. The capital value of the trust is now over $5 million, and over $7 million has been distributed.

The singer June Bronhill won *The Sun* aria contest in 1950. Her real name was June Gough but she adopted the name Bronhill as a contracted version of her home town, Broken Hill (N.S.W.).

Dorothea Mackellar's fiercely Australian poem "My Country", was first published in England, not in Australia, in 1908. It made its first appearance in the London *Spectator*.

The first Australian to win an American Academy Award was the war photographer Damien Parer. His brilliant film was put together by Cinesound to make the award-winning *Kokoda Front Line*. Parer was later killed in action.

The ballad "The Wild Colonial Boy" describes the exploits and eventual capture of Jack Doolan, Jack Duggan, Jack Dowling or Jack Donovan. The real person described was a young bushranger called Jack Donahoe, who was finally shot dead at Campbelltown (N.S.W.) in 1830.

Ava Gardner said it all when she was in Melbourne for the filming of *On the Beach*, a movie about the end of the world. Not particularly thrilled with the lack of activity, she said—"I couldn't imagine a better place for the making of a film on the end of the world."

The actor Leo McKern who still bumbles about on television as "Rumpole of the Bailey" was a commercial artist for a while before becoming an actor. He was born at Petersham in Sydney in 1920.

The biggest-selling Australian book of all time is *The Commonsense Cookery Book*, produced by the New South Wales Cookery Association. The biggest-selling work of fiction is *The Magic Pudding* by Norman Lindsay.

THE ARTS

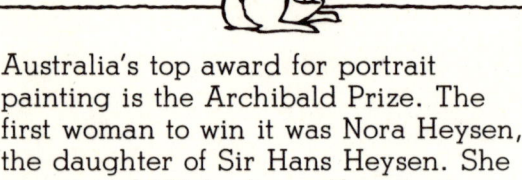

Australia's top award for portrait painting is the Archibald Prize. The first woman to win it was Nora Heysen, the daughter of Sir Hans Heysen. She won it in 1938 for her self portrait.

Rolf Boldrewood (Thomas Alexander Browne) (1826-1915), author of *Robbery Under Arms* and other books, was a squatter with a run on the Murrumbidgee River. The severe droughts of 1866-1869 drove him from the land, and he became a magistrate, a goldfields commissioner and finally a writer.

In the gold rush era Australia's greatest amusement park, the Disneyland of the 1850s, was Cremorne Gardens in the Melbourne suburb of Richmond. It was situated near the present intersection of Punt Road and the South-eastern Freeway, where the elegant grain silos now stand.

The Heidelberg School of painters produced some of Australia's best landscape work. However, they were together in Heidelberg only for about two years, from 1888 to 1890, when they decided to go their own ways. Notwithstanding this they had an immense influence on Australian art.

In the early years of the *Bulletin*, "Banjo" Paterson and Henry Lawson had an ongoing "feud". Paterson thought that Lawson's verse was much too gloomy and should portray a brighter side of Australian life. Lawson charged Paterson with not treating outback suffering with enough seriousness. Paterson later revealed that the "feud", which was conducted in verse published by the *Bulletin*, was a hoax he and Lawson had conspired at together.

Australian author M. Barnard Eldershaw was really two people who wrote together—Marjorie Faith Barnard and Flora Eldershaw. Marjorie Barnard also wrote several books alone.

The cast iron decoration in Victorian era houses (often wrongly called wrought iron), was a feature of houses in Sydney and Melbourne. Designs were patented by manufacturers in each city and consequently there are subtle differences between the iron in the two cities.

The first play about Australia was probably *Les Emigres aux Terres Australes*, a play based on the travels of French navigator La Perouse. It was produced in Paris in 1792.

Louis Buvelot (1814-1888) is regarded as the father of Australian landscape painting. He was born and trained in Switzerland and lived in Brazil for 18 years before coming to live in Australia in 1865. He worked as a photographer in Melbourne. His painting was not particularly well regarded by art critics of the day.

One of the earliest uses made of film in Australia was in the Salvation Army's spectacular *Soldiers of the Cross* (1900), a four-hour combination of film, slides, music and sermons. It could not, however, claim to be Australia's first feature film because the film was used only as one part of the proceedings.

Popular modern Australian artist Pro Hart's real name is Kevin Charles Hart. When he worked in the Broken Hill mines after leaving school his creative activities in inventing and painting earned him the title of professor (Pro for short). When he became a full-time artist he retained the nickname.

THE ARTS

Children's Books too Good to Miss

The following lists are for young people aged 8–14 years. The criteria used to compile the lists were:

1. Recognised literary quality and proven child appeal.
2. A story which has something worthwhile to say in the sense of a theme worth caring about.
3. A memorable quality.
4. Range of genres, e.g. realism, fantasy, history, science fiction.
5. Range of literary styles and techniques, e.g. diary, first person narrative, flashback, time slip, alternating dialogue.
6. Authors whose included works may entice a reader to search for others by the same author.
7. Australian flavour (though there are some exceptions).

Australian Books

Aldridge, James
The True Story of Lillie Stubeck, 1984
Balderson, Margaret
When Jays Fly to Barbmo, 1970
Brinsmead, Hesba
Longtime Passing, 1971
Brinsmead, Hesba
Pastures of the Blue Crane, 1966
Chauncy, Nan
Tangara, 1960
Clark, Mavis Thorpe
The Min-Min, 1966
French, Simon
Cannily, Cannily, 1981
Gleeson, Libby
Eleanor, Elizabeth, 1984
Harding, Lee
Displaced Person, 1979
Kelleher, Victor
Master of the Grove, 1982
Klein, Robin
Penny Pollard's Diary, 1983
Martin, David
Cabby's Daughter, 1974
Ottley, Reginald
By the Sandhills of Yamboorah, 1965

Park, Ruth
Callie's Castle, 1974
Park, Ruth
Playing Beattie Bow, 1980
Phipson, Joan
A Tide Flowing, 1981
Phipson, Joan
The Watcher in the Garden, 1982
Scott, Bill
Boorie, 1978
Southall, Ivan
Josh, 1971
Spence, Eleanor
The October Child, 1976
Stow, Randolph
Midnite: The Story of a Wild Colonial Boy, 1967
Thiele, Colin
The Fire in the Stone, 1974
Thiele, Colin
Storm-Boy, 1963
Wrightson, Patricia
I Own the Racecourse!, 1968
Wrightson, Patricia
The Nargun and the Stars, 1974

Other Books

Adams, Richard
Watership Down, 1974
Alexander, Lloyd
The Prydain Chronicles.
First title: *The Book of Three*, 1964
Babbitt, Natalie
Tuck Everlasting, 1975
Blume, Judy
Are You There, God? It's Me, Margaret, 1970
Bond, Michael
A Bear Called Paddington, 1960
Boston, Lucy
The Children of Green Knowe, 1955
Byars, Betsy
The Eighteenth Emergency, 1973
Cleary, Beverly
The *Ramona* books. First title: *Ramona the Pest*, 1968
Cooper, Susan
The Dark is Rising sequence. First title: *Over Sea, Under Stone*, 1965

THE ARTS

Cormier, Robert
The Chocolate War, 1974
Dahl, Roald
Charlie and the Chocolate Factory, 1964
Fitzhugh, Louise
Harriet the Spy, 1964
Frank, Anne
Anne Frank: The Diary of a Young Girl, 1952
Garner, Alan
The Owl Service, 1968
Le Guin, Ursula
The *Earthsea* trilogy. First title: *The Wizard of Earthsea*, 1968
Lewis, C. S.
The Chronicles of Narnia. First title: *The Lion, the Witch, and the Wardrobe*, 1950
O'Brien, Robert
Mrs Frisby and the Rats of Nimh, 1971
Norton, Mary
The *Borrowers* series. First title: *The Borrowers*, 1952.
Paterson, Katherine
Bridge to Terabithia, 1977
Pearce, Philippa
Tom's Midnight Garden, 1959
Tolkien, J. R. R.
The Hobbit, 1937
Townsend, Sue
The Secret Diary of Adrian Mole Aged 13¾, 1982
White, E. B.
Charlotte's Web, 1952
Wilder, Laura Ingalls
The *Little House* series. First title: *Little House in the Big Woods*, 1932
Zindel, Paul
The Pigman, 1968

AUSTRALIAN CHILDREN'S BOOK AWARD WINNERS

From 1946 until 1950, the Australian Children's Book Awards were issued by the Australian Book Society and between 1951 and 1956, by the Children's Book Council of New South Wales. In 1957, judges from the Children's Book Council of Victoria were appointed, followed in 1958 by judges from South Australia. In 1958, the Children's Book Council of Australia, representing all States, was formed and has administered these awards since 1959.

- **1946** • Leslie Rees *Karrawingi the Emu*
- **1947** • no award
- **1948** • Frank Hurley *Shackleton's Argonauts* (non-fiction)
- **1949** • Alan Villiers *Whalers of the Midnight Sun*
- **1950** • no award
- **1951** • Ruth Williams *Verity of Sydney Town*
- **1952** • Eve Pownall *The Australia Book* (non-fiction)
- **1953** • Joan Phipson *Good Luck to the Rider*
  J. H. & W. D. Martin *Aircraft of Today and Tomorrow* (non-fiction)
- **1954** • K. Langloh Parker *Australian Legendary Tales*
- **1955** • N. B. Tindale & H. A. Lindsay *The First Walkabout* (non-fiction)
- **1956** • Patricia Wrightson *The Crooked Snake*
- **1957** • Enid Moodie-Heddle (Ed.) *The Boomerang Book of Legendary Tales*
- **1958** • Nan Chauncy *Tiger in the Bush*
- **1959** • Nan Chauncy *Devil's Hill*
  John Gunn *Sea Menace*
- **1960** • Kylie Tennant *All the Proud Tribesmen*
- **1961** • Nan Chauncy *Tangara*
- **1962** • L. H. Evers *The Racketty Street Gang*
  Joan Woodberry *Rafferty Rides a Winner*
- **1963** • Joan Phipson *The Family Conspiracy*
- **1964** • Eleanor Spence *The Green Laurel*
- **1965** • Hesba Brinsmead *Pastures of the Blue Crane*
- **1966** • Ivan Southall *Ash Road*
- **1967** • Mavis Thorpe Clark *The Min-Min*
- **1968** • Ivan Southall *To the Wild Sky*
- **1969** • Margaret Balderson *When Jays Fly to Barbmo*
- **1970** • Annette Macarthur-Onslow *Uhu*
- **1971** • Ivan Southall *Bread and Honey*

THE ARTS

- 1972 • Hesba Brinsmead *Longtime Passing*
- 1973 • Noreen Shelley *Family at the Lookout*
- 1974 • Patricia Wrightson *The Nargun and the Stars*
- 1975 • no award
- 1976 • Ivan Southall *Fly West* (non-fiction)
- 1977 • Eleanor Spence *The October Child*
- 1978 • Patricia Wrightson *The Ice is Coming*
- 1979 • Ruth Manley *The Plum Rain Scroll*
- 1980 • Lee Harding *Displaced Person*
- 1981 • Ruth Park *Playing Beattie Bow*
- 1982 • Colin Thiele *The Valley Between*
- 1983 • Victor Kelleher *Master of the Grove*
- 1984 • Patricia Wrightson *A Little Fear*
- 1985 • James Aldridge *The True Story of Lilli Stubeck*

INDEPENDENT MUSIC IN AUSTRALIA

Independent music in Australia covers a wide variety of different styles, ranging from hardcore punk to country music, each with its own following, fashion and lifestyle.

The punk explosion of the late 1970s broke down the way people thought about popular music and it became quite acceptable to explore all musical avenues, even to the extent of changing them radically from their original form to create a new genus.

As the shock waves of punk began to die down, people started looking for other musical outlets through which they could express what they heard, felt and saw. This led on the one hand, to a plundering of music history for inspiration. On the other, people began looking more closely at their environment in search for a new direction, experimenting with a variety of instruments and objects in order to capture what they experienced.

In Australia, the most popular style has been a post-**Birthday Party** mutation of rock'n'roll. Any doubts that this is so will be quickly dispelled by a visit to an inner-city rock venue. The style played there has been called "swamp", a combination of a number of different elements, among them sixties garage band psychedelia, rockabilly, country music and punk. The country influence can best be seen in the *Beasts of Bourbon* cover of the black-humour-fuelled country song *Psycho*. The sound itself is very guitar-dominated, anchored solidly with a combination of drums and electric bass guitars. Some bands have adopted a **Cramps**-style of attack with two electric guitars, drums, harmonica and an almost screaming style of slide guitar, used to add colour to the music. The **Cramps** are an American band which has been called one of the founders of "swamp".

It is, however, the vocals which give "swamp" its individuality. A dark, almost primal scream is used, not only to deliver the words, but to express a number of emotions such as fear and sorrow, or to give the overall sound a haunting, sinister feel.

When talking about "swamp", it is impossible not to mention the now-disbanded **Birthday Party**, one of the most successful rock'n'roll bands Australia has produced. Their influence has extended to England, Europe and the U.S.A., and has been so widespread that any new band working within the genre cannot escape the inevitable **Birthday Party** comparisons.

The **Birthday Party** took rock'n'roll in totally new directions, receiving critical acclaim overseas and charting well in a number of independent charts

THE ARTS

before they broke up following an Australian tour in 1983.

Nick Cave, former lead singer of **The Birthday Party**, survived the break-up of the band and has since embarked upon a solo career. Freed from the constraints of the band, Cave plunged headlong into a world inhabited by nightmares, only touched upon in his earlier work. Assuming the skin of a rotting nightclub singer, he attacks with the ferocity of a betrayed lover. An artist balancing on the edge of a chasm, he is able to manipulate his image until he becomes a parody of himself.

The music is best described as a sparse, almost "blues" scream, giving most of his work a violent, knife-like edge and often making it an uncomfortable experience to listen to (very often his intention). *From Here to Eternity* and *The First Born is Dead* (the latter's title being a reference to Elvis whose twin brother was born dead) are lyrically Cave's most ambitious works to date. Both show a fascination for the American south, ranging from *Saint Huck* who is corrupted by the big city, to *Knocking on Joe*, a term used by prisoners in the U.S. for the practice of self-mutilation to gain a respite from hard labour.

With his band **The Bad Seeds** (which contains another ex-**Birthday Party** member, Mick Harvey), Nick Cave has toured the U.K., Europe and the U.S. He is once again set to slither across the stages of this country. Like Raskolnikov in Dostoyevsky's *Crime and Punishment*, he coughs into his handkerchief and displays the spots for all to see.

Another **Birthday Party** splinter is **Crime and the City Solution**, featuring Roland Howard and, once again, Mick Harvey. They follow more closely the dark footsteps of their previous band, and have released one E.P., *The Dangling Man*, which has received a mixed reception from the public and music press.

Salamander Jim is another band which fell into the "swamp", fuelled by the drunken visions of lead singer, Tex Perkins. Allusions to a world inhabited by drunken rednecks, rampaging nightmares and cowboy mythology are delivered with a "country growl" vocal style. Although no longer with us, they have left behind a mini-album with the ominous title *Lorne Green Shares His Precious Fluids*. (Surely not the grey side-burned patriarch of *Bonanza*?)

In Europe, Tex attempted to create a new band, to be called **The Fur Bible**, with ex-members of **The Gun Club**. He has returned to Australia to form a new band with some ex-members of **Salamander Jim** which has the working name, **The Butcher Shop**. New material has been recorded, but at the time of writing has not been released.

The Scientists are another "swamp" monster. They have often been described in the musical press as a "cartoon band". Just as a cartoon is an exaggeration of life, the band's image and music (garage band psychedelia and swamp) is blown up to larger-than-life proportions. Assisted by a rhythm section of avalanche proportions, screaming blues and slide guitar are combined with primal vocals to produce a post-apocalypse vision of rock'n'roll. This is another band which, owing to the limited scope of the Australian music circuit and mixed reception from the public, ventured overseas in search of success and found it. Their *Blood Red River* mini-album was selected as one of last year's Albums of the Year by the English magazine *Sounds*. The band have just released a "best of" album with the descriptive title *Heading for a Trauma*, a rare achievement for an Australian independent band.

THE ARTS

Another band which has created quite a good reputation in the U.K. are **The Moodists**. Theirs is a very primitive sound, creating a nightmare world of sex, fast cars and demented alcoholic visions, further emphasised by a thundering back-beat. The band returned to the U.K. earlier this year after a short tour of this country, gaining, at best, a mixed reception from the press and public.

Crashing somewhere between "power pop" and a "Detroit sound" are **The Hoodoo Gurus**. Originally a line-up consisting of three electric guitars and drums, the band began to attract the inevitable **Cramps** comparisons. Now incorporating bass and dropping one guitar, their songs have become more traditional in form, exhibiting an ever-increasing sixties influence. This is reflected in their appearance—a mutated sixties garage-band style, combined with simple catchy lyrics which deal with themes as diverse as necrophilia and lost love.

Last year the band completed a short, successful tour of the U.S., a country with which they have strong affiliations. Their debut album, *Stoneage Romeos*, and their second, *Mars Needs Guitars*, have gone gold—a major achievement for an independent band in this country. Watch out! The hair is longer, the paisley brighter and the car is full of fuel.

"Swamp" fashion is a strange brew of exaggerated rockabilly quiffs, punk leather and studs, cowboy fashion and religious symbols, with a touch of late seventies glitter thrown in to give the mixture added spice.

A music style currently going through a strong resurgence is rockabilly. It never completely disappeared, having retained an extremely loyal following since its beginnings. Not only has it retained this original following, it has attracted a legion of new fans. Its appeal has become timeless and cuts across age barriers.

Rockabilly strips back emotions to the basics, concentrating on themes dealing with love, fast cars and a variety of heroes. It is a melting pot of gospel, blues and country music played with a combination of acoustic or semi-acoustic guitars, double bass, percussion and sometimes, piano.

There are a number of rockabilly bands currently playing the traps, the most prominent being **The Milky Bar Kids**. Others are **The Eddys, The Blue Caps** (all the members actually wear blue caps) and **Wild Cat Tamers**.

The strength of devotion to this style of music can be seen in rockabilly fashions. Gear includes full skirts, bobbysox (short white socks), quiffs (turned-up fringe style haircuts), long jackets (which sometimes have painted on them anything from Confederate flags to emblems which would not have looked out of place on a U.S. World War II bomber), ripple-soled shoes, jeans, white T-shirts and baggy-trousered suits.

Another important aspect of rockabilly is dancing. It has often been described as a type of "throw your partner" aerobics which, like the music and the fashion, has not changed with the years. Though originally favoured by the working-class, it now attracts a strong middle-class audience.

A style common to the "jungles" of Sydney is the "post-**Radio Birdman**" sound. Heavily influenced by the late sixties/early seventies style originated by the Detroit bands **M.C.5** and **The Stooges**, it is a combination of fast, guitar-driven, hard rock and power pop. Traditional to a large extent, it combines an almost adolescent view of society with a strong sense of humour. There is also a decided television

THE ARTS

influence. Most of the bands have adopted a strong anti-fashion stance, concentrating on the traditional rock uniform of jeans, T-shirts, sneakers and leather jackets.

Celibate Rifles (the name being a send-up of **The Sex Pistols**), is a band which has achieved some success within this genre, having also gained attention in a number of English music publications. Two factors distinguish this band from the others. One, it is based in the upper middle-class area of Sydney's North Shore and, two, it is prepared to comment on a variety of social issues including the problems created by an ever-increasing suburbia.

The Monkees meet Godzilla could be an apt description of Adelaide band **Eastern Dark** (a name which has links with the *Phantom* comic strip). Their songs are short, fast and tight, with entertainment high on their list of priorities. This Detroit-fuelled monster is currently making inroads into the eastern States due partly to the success of their single *Julie is a Junkie*.

Countless T-shirts declare that punk is not dead and from all appearances punk still has a substantial cult following. Punk music is comprised of short songs which are played at a very fast, aggressive speed. Lasting no more than two to three minutes, and very often containing no more than two to three basic chords, it is a kind of rock'n'roll "blitzkrieg" with all the manners of a rampaging tank.

The main philosophy of punk is anarchy, although this has become open to conflicting interpretations. The older punks, who were present during the genre's chaotic birth in the seventies, view it as people searching for humanity and non-violence, whereas the younger punks look upon it in the context of getting drunk, seeing bands and generally enjoying yourself. The main meeting place for punks in Sydney continues to be the Paddington markets, where they will pose for photos for a small fee and find out about parties and where their favourite bands are playing. *Sydney From the Sewer* is one of the few fanzines which is written by punks for punks.

Punk fashion is a mixture of severely-spiked and mohawk-styled hair, leather jackets (sometimes covered in a large number of studs), studded wrist bands, bondage trousers and straight-legged jeans, badges, sewn-on patches and military-style boots.

A new storm appears to be brewing in suburban Sydney and at its centre may be seen **The Hard Ons** and **Itchy Rat**. **The Hard Ons** are a group of suburban outlaws whose "no holds barred" attitude has already alienated many in the music industry. They are hard, fast and funny; any band which includes in their set list a song entitled "Surfing on My Face", has to have a sense of humour. Their songs accurately reflect the suburban environment they grew up in.

Itchy Rat is a band determined to play the game its own way. Their songs, dealing with such diverse themes as drugs (*Attempting to Give Your Name To A Policeman While Tripping*), bombs and the problems faced by the suburban family. You can hear a collage of musical influences in their music, ranging from reggae to hard core punk. As the S.A.S. motto states, "He Who Dares, Wins".

Box of Fish, on the other hand, was a band with its feet firmly planted in "gothic punk". With a stage backdrop of old horror movies, the band was a writhing monster of distorted guitars and thundering rhythms. Though the monster is now dead, the ghost can be heard on the *Slap 'Em Around the Gills* album.

An invitation to "come with me on a strange journey through the past"

THE ARTS  13

could be used to summarise the psychedelia revival. Once again a group of young bands is looking back to the sixties, searching for direction and inspiration while attracting an ever-increasing audience eager to experience something which they were too young to remember in its original form. Musically, it is a bright collage of swirling keyboards and jangling, screaming guitars, combined with a solid backbeat which attacks not only the mind, but the feet as well. Lyrically, it is a blend of surrealistic (some would say drug-induced) images, as well as the more traditional rock themes.

A band which has been given the psychedelic label is **The Crystal Set**. Looking like they stepped out of a documentary on psychedelia, circa California 1967, the band presents a kaleidoscope of visual and sound imagery. A feature of their performances is a backdrop which can feature at any one time (or simultaneously) surrealist paintings, splashes of colour, photographs and pages from reference books.

Representing English psychedelia are **Surprise Surprise**. Though their music has a slightly harder edge, they are sometimes reminiscent of the Syd Barrett-era **Pink Floyd**. They also incorporate a slide show in their performance, using coloured oil to create a series of swirling patterns. (It is not as visually dominant as the slides used by **The Crystal Set**.)

Other bands working within this genre include **The Moffs** (a mating of U.K. and U.S. psychedelia), **The Psychotic Turnbuckles** and **The Acid Drops**.

A tradition in contemporary music culture is fashion used as an extension of the music to give it a readily-identifiable image. Psychedelia is no different. It is a combination of bright paisley designs, jeans (even better if patched with brightly-coloured material), pointed toe boots or pixie boots, beads, various military jackets and long hair. It can be seen as a natural progression of the "mod" subculture.

The Triffids is a band which has responded to the challenge of overseas success and achieved it, gaining critical and public acclaim in the U.K. Originating in Perth, the same birthplace as **The Scientists** (but that is where all comparisons end), their sound comprises a bright, melodic top which is firmly anchored by a strong rhythm section. Although it was thought that the ghost of Jim Morrison was hovering over the band, these fears were quickly dispelled. Owing more to sixties folk rock and late seventies "New York new wave" than the English punk explosion, the band still includes a number of cover versions in its repertoire. They are also one of the few acts to have used their influences to create a unique sound.

THE ARTS

Hunters and Collectors, one of the larger working bands in the country, gives us a thundering heartbeat and vision which captures the qualities of a land as large and culturally diverse as Australia. The band has a strong rhythm section incorporating a marked tribal feeling which invites the body to move with it. This is used in conjunction with brass, guitar and synthesiser to give the sound a haunting urban quality — a quality intended to accurately reflect modern Australia.

Hunters and Collectors populate their lyrics with mad truck drivers and surrealistic images of Australian life and scenery. Their *Jawes of Life* album is based around an incident in the Northern Territory where a truck was driven into a crowded hotel. Many critics have stated that the band are at their best on stage, something which has prompted the release of a live album and video, both entitled *The Way To Go Out*. **Hunters and Collectors** have toured overseas to critical, if not commercial, success. This could have something to do with the uniquely Australian feel that the band has captured, something to which overseas audiences may have difficulty in relating.

Australian contemporary music has traditionally been the bastion of the white male, but recent years have seen the emergence of a number of Aboriginal bands, in particular, **The Warumpi Band, Coloured Stone** and **Mantaka**. The Warumpi Band has its base in the Northern Territory and its music is a combination of rhythm and blues, rock'n'roll and country music. An interesting aspect of the band's style is its use of Aboriginal instruments. Fired by a sense of fun and a strong, danceable rhythm, The Warumpi Band tours Aboriginal settlements of the Northern Territory as well as major Australian cities. They have also toured the United Kingdom and the South Pacific region, including such exotic locations as Guadalcanal — areas that are not generally considered by touring bands.

Mantaka is a band from the north of Queensland. It has a rock'n'roll sound similar to **The Rolling Stones** of 1973, incorporating an additional reggae feel.

The plight of Aboriginal rock bands in this country was graphically portrayed in the film *Wrong Side of the Road* which depicts two bands, **No Fixed Address** and **Us Mob**, following them through confrontations with the police and the general problems of just finding somewhere to play.

Surprisingly few white Australian bands have explored the rich musical heritage of Aboriginal music that is lying just outside their door, preferring to look towards the United States and United Kingdom for inspiration.

There are a number of people who are not to content to work within the basic contemporary music format of drums, guitars and keyboards and have bravely decided to strike out in more "obscure" directions. One such band is **Severed Heads** now living in self-imposed exile in Great Britain. Electronic experimentalists, they use such instruments as a keyboard bass (an uncommon instrument in Australian bands), computers, a vocoder (an instrument which dramatically alters the user's voice), synthesisers and video technology. The band has recently returned to tour Australia.

P.S.J. is a group of tribal junkmen who will use anything that makes a sound. They mix conventional drums, guitar and synthesiser with pieces of metal, hubcaps and the rims of bicycle wheels to produce a sound which creates images of a decaying urban landscape.

Madroom is a band which, for

THE ARTS

better or worse, has dived headfirst into the black areas which can be found in the depths of everyone's heart. Their lyrics are littered with almost blasphemous religious imagery drawing on the darker side of the sixties to create sound which can both entertain and disturb those who gather to listen. An interesting aspect of **Madroom**'s sound is the use of such things as a toy piano, a metal garden seat and a screeching violin to give the music an eerie, almost nightmarish quality.

Shower Scene From Psycho is a strange conglomeration of sixties pop and eighties synthesiser technology. Bouncing out of Melbourne with their tongues firmly planted in their cheeks, the band brings a breath of fresh air to independent music, plus something which it has lacked for a long time—a sense of humour.

Some groups are redefining what a musical instrument is and how it should be used. One such band is **S.P.K.** which, after a less than favourable reception from Australian audiences, removed itself to England. Theirs is an industrial sound, created with metal drums, various pieces of metal (which are attacked with a variety of hammers) and electric saws. These are substituted for conventional percussion instruments and are used in conjunction with a synthesiser and electric bass guitar. This is further combined with a primitive form of performance art. The group's sound has already had a strong influence and can be heard in the music of England's **Test Department**, the West German band **Collapsing New Buildings** and Australia's already mentioned **P.S.J.**

A musical style which underwent a strong rebirth in the late seventies and now seems to be on the increase again is the "mod phenomenon" of the early sixties soul and Motown and of English bands such as **The Who** and **The Small Faces**. A main feature of mod music is the guitar style, which is dominated by the use of power chords and single note playing. Its main theme deals with the celebration of youth and all its joys and heartbreaks, combining this with a sometimes naive social conscience.

Fashion plays an important part within mod cultures. The best-dressed, most respected members are given the title "Ace Face". Mods dress themselves in smart, three-buttoned suits, thin ties, Army-disposal parkas (often decorated with a large variety of sewn-on patches depicting such heroes as **The Who** and **The Jam**), miniskirts and ski pants, and sport neat French and Cilla Black-style haircuts. They ride scooters which are usually adorned with a number of rear-vision mirrors.

There is only a small number of mod bands working in Australia. A large void was created by the demise of **Fast Cars**, which was looked upon as the premier band of this type. The Go is something which occurs at the Sydney Trade Union Club on Saturday nights; its popularity can be fathomed by the number of mods who gather outside the club's doors on those nights.

Scattered Order is a band which sometimes takes its inspiration from the ugly side of life, with a sound which can be likened to a shuddering collision of heavy funk and rock'n'roll. They have often appeared to be the perfect band to listen to while watching a car crash. But it seems that this may have changed with the appearance of that thing called "melody" on their new album *Career of the Silly Thing*. Their music sometimes appeared as though it had been searching for direction; perhaps now it has found it. The band is once again back on the live circuit and is touring the land with **Severed Heads**.

The independent industry itself has been largely ignored by the major radio stations which seem to be hoping that it

will dry up and blow away. One of the major stumbling blocks to public acceptance is image. It was during the late 1970s punk explosion that a number of independent labels were founded. They evolved from record stores and groups of friends coming together to cater to an audience which wanted a certain kind of music that was not being provided by the major labels. The majority of them adopted a do-it-yourself philosophy, the results of which varied in quality from very good to extremely bad. This inconsistency turned a number of people away from the music. Although most of the product is now of a consistently high standard, the stigma still exists.

What of the future of this type of music? As the cost of producing records increases, independent labels are not in a strong enough financial position to experiment and concentrate on a sound or band which has the potential to net them a substantial return. This can lead to stagnation in the music itself as bands are not prepared to risk experimenting to any great extents.

September 1st, 1985 saw the introduction of the New South Wales Liquor Administration Board's new fire regulations, something which could prove to be a virtual stake in the heart for independent music in Sydney. While Sydney has long prided itself on the large number of clubs and hotels which promote live music, over the last 12 months a large percentage of venues have been forced to either renovate their premises or cease operating as live music venues.

This does not bode well for the future of independent music.

Countdown Award Winners

The listings below relate to the year of the achievement and not to the year in which the awards were presented. Award titles may change from year to year and are not necessarily employed each time.

1979
Most Popular Female Performer:
Christie Allen
Most Popular Male Performer:
Jon English
Most Popular Group:
Little River Band
Best Australian Single:
Mi-Sex, "Computer Games"
Best Australian Album:
Little River Band, "First Under the Wire"
Most Outstanding Achievement in Australian Music:
Little River Band

Best New Talent:
Mi-Sex
Best Producer:
Peter Dawkins (Mi-Sex)
Best Australian Songwriter:
Terry Britten (Goose Bumps)
Best Album Cover Design:
"Breakfast at Sweethearts"
Countdown Producers Award (for continued co-operation, enthusiasm and professionalism):
The Angels
Most Popular Deejays:
Ian McRae (Sydney) Greg Evans (Melbourne) Yorkie (Perth) Wayne Roberts (Brisbane) Steve Curtis (Adelaide) Tim Franklin (Hobart)

1980
Most Popular Female Performer:
Christie Allen

THE ARTS

Most Popular Male Performer:
James Reyne (Australian Crawl)
Most Popular Australian Group:
Cold Chisel
Most Popular Australian Record:
Cold Chisel, "East"
Best Australian Single Record: *Split Enz, "I Got You"*
Best Australian Album: *Cold Chisel, "East"*
Best Australian Recorded Songwriter: *Don Walker of Cold Chisel*
Best Australian Record Producer: *Mark Opitz*
Best Australian Record Cover: *Cold Chisel, "East"*
Most Outstanding Achievement in Australian Music (for excellence in the presentation or production of Australian rock music by an individual performer, group or group member):
Cold Chisel
Most Popular Deejays:
Ian McRae (Sydney—2SM) Greg Evans (Melbourne—3XY) Wayne Roberts (Brisbane—4BK) Gary Shannon (Perth—6PM) Steve Curtis (Adelaide—5AD) Tim Franklin (Hobart—7HT)
Johnny O'Keefe Memorial Award for the Best New Talent (individual or group):
Flowers

1981
Most Popular Female:
Sharon O'Neill
Most Popular Male:
James Reyne
Most Popular Group:
Australian Crawl
Best Single:
Mental As Anything, "If You Leave Me Can I Come Too"
Best Album:
Mondo Rock, "Chemistry"
Best Debut Single:
Men At Work, "Who Can It Be Now"
Best Debut Album:
Men At Work, "Business As Usual"
Most Promising New Talent:
Men At Work

Best Songwriter:
Eric McCusker (Mondo Rock)
Best Consistent Live Act:
Cold Chisel
Best Producer:
Peter Dawkins
Most Outstanding Achievement:
Air Supply

1982
Most Popular Female Performer:
Christina Amphlett
Most Popular Male Performer:
Iva Davies
Most Popular Group:
Split Enz
Most Popular International Act:
Duran Duran
Best Single:
Moving Pictures, "What About Me"
Best Album:
Split Enz, "Time and Tide"
Best Debut Single:
Goanna, "Solid Rock"
Best Debut Album:
Goanna, "Spirit of Place"
Most Promising New Talent:
Goanna
Most Outstanding Achievement:
Men At Work
Best Songwriter:
Tim Finn
Best Producer:
Mark Opitz

1983
Most Popular Female Performer:
Sharon O'Neill
Most Popular Male Performer:
Tim Finn
Most Popular Group:
Australian Crawl
Most Popular International Act:
Duran Duran
The Johnny O'Keefe Award for the Most Promising New Talent:
Real Life
Best Debut Single:
Pat Wilson, "Bop Girl"

THE ARTS

Best Debut Album:
Real Life, "Heartland"
Best Recorded Songwriter:
Tim Finn
Best Record Producer:
Mark Moffatt and Ricky Fataar
Best Single:
Midnight Oil, "Power and the Passion"
Best Album:
Tim Finn, "Escapade"
Most Outstanding Achievement:
Men At Work
Best Promotional Video:
*"Fraction Too Much Friction",
Tim Finn—produced by
Richard Lowenstein*

1984
Most Popular Female Performer:
Sharon O'Neill
Most Popular Male Performer:
Michael Hutchence
Most Popular Australian Group:
INXS
Most Popular International Group:
Duran Duran
Best Debut Single:
I'm Talking, "Trust Me"
Best Debut Album:
Hoodoo Gurus, "Stoneage Romeos"
Most Popular New Talent:
I'm Talking
Best Songwriter:
Farris/Hutchence
Best Producer:
Martin Armiger
Best Single:
*Eurogliders,
"Heaven (Must Be There)"*
Best Album:
INXS, "The Swing"
Most Outstanding Achievement:
INXS
Best Female Performance in a Video:
Sharon O'Neill
Best Male Performance in a Video:
Jimmy Barnes
Best Group Performance in a Video:
INXS, "Burn for You"
Best Video (tie):
*"Apocolypso", Mental As
Anything—produced by "B" Sharp
Productions
"Burn for You", INXS—produced
by Richard Lowenstein*

1985
Most Popular Australian Female
Performer:
Kate Ceberano
Most Popular Australian Male Performer:
Michael Hutchence
Most Popular Australian Group:
INXS
Most Popular International Act (non-Australian):
Duran Duran
Most Promising New Talent:
Do. Ré Mi.
Best Debut Single:
Do. Ré Mi., "Man Overboard"
Best Debut Album:
Do. Ré Mi., "Domestic Harmony"
Best Songwriter:
"Greedy" Smith
Best Producer:
Mark Opitz
Best Single (tie):
*Models, "Out of Mind Out of Sight"
Mental as Anything, "Live It Up"*
Best Album:
Mental as Anything, "Fundamental"
Most Outstanding Achievement (tie):
*Oz for Africa
INXS*
Best Female Performance in a Video:
Christina Amphlett, "Pleasure and Pain"
Best Male Performance in a Video:
Jimmy Barnes, "Working Class Man"
Best Group Performance in a Video:
Mental as Anything, "Live It Up"
Best Video:
*"What You Need",
INXS—produced by
INXS/Richard Lowenstein*

The National Music Camp Association

The National Music Camp Association was formed in 1948 by the late Professor John Bishop to give young people the opportunity to play orchestral music together. At that time few youth orchestral opportunities existed outside of the music institutions. The aim of the founders was for young instrumentalists to help each other develop as musicians and as people, to discover more beauties in the music they make, and to develop friendships based on shared musical experiences.

Camp is now held in two weeks of January, when over three hundred of the best young orchestral musicians in Australia, between the ages of 14 and 22, chosen by audition, assemble for intensive tutorials and rehearsals in the major works of the orchestral repertoire. The top professional orchestral musicians give their services as tutors, and the National Music Camp engages excellent conductors for the four ensembles that are formed. The camps, which are usually held in a major boarding school, also combine the many elements of a holiday, so that the national camp is the highlight of the year for many young musicians.

The music camp movement has expanded now to incorporate local music camps, usually held in the winter vacation, in Sydney, Albury, Melbourne, Hobart, Adelaide and Perth. In this way, an ever-growing number of young musicians have the opportunity to participate, the State camps providing a training ground for many who proceed to the national camp.

THE ARTS

THE AUSTRALIAN YOUTH ORCHESTRA

Such was the success of National Music Camp in the 1950s that in 1957, the first season of the Australian Youth Orchestra was convened. This orchestra, comprising 100 young musicians between the ages of 15 and 22, chosen from all over Australia, was immediately hailed as a new, vital force in Australian music. Since then, the A.Y.O. has grown in experience and stature, giving concerts each year in various cities of Australia. Playing an increasingly demanding repertoire, the programming of the A.Y.O. now reflects that of the top professional orchestras.

In 1970, the A.Y.O. undertook its first overseas tour and performed at the Expo in Osaka. Subsequent tours have taken the orchestra to Asia in 1975, America for the Bicentennial in 1976 and to China in 1979. Nineteen eighty-four saw the A.Y.O. undertake its most demanding and prestigious tour when it made a five week tour of Europe, playing at major music festivals. It was widely acclaimed as the highlight of the Edinburgh Festival, and the A.Y.O.'s Prom concert in the Royal Albert Hall saw a capacity audience of 7500 give a rousing and prolonged ovation to this talented orchestra. The British and European music critics acclaimed the A.Y.O. as possibly the finest youth orchestra in the world.

To find out more about the music camp movement, contact: The Administrator, National Music Camp Association, 19 North Terrace, Adelaide, S.A. 5069.

DANCE

If you're good on your toes, artistically inclined, attracted to the bright lights or just want to keep fit, then dancing is for you.

Potential ballet dancers need to start at an early age; some start as young as three. The way to enter a State dance company is to build up technique and experience with one of the many private ballet schools in each State. To begin with, the budding dancer would only have one hourly session a week, increasing to a couple of daily sessions from the age of twelve onwards. From the age of about fifteen, you have to be very serious about your dancing career because from then on the course becomes full-time. Each year there are examinations where you have to prove your abilities before moving on to a more advanced level. There are tertiary courses available in most States and each State has its own dance company which dancers join only after strenuous auditions. It is hard work, but don't be put off, there are good times to be had along the way.

Below is a list of State ballet companies. Get in contact with them to find a reputable ballet teacher near you.

New South Wales
Sydney Dance Company,
36 Bourke Street, Woolloomooloo 2011.
Tel. (02) 358 4600.

Victoria
The Australian Ballet,
11 Mt Alexander Road, Flemington 3031.
Tel. (03) 376 1400.

South Australia
Adelaide Dance Company,
The Dance Centre, 25 Whitmore Sq.
Adelaide 5000.
Tel (08) 212 1665.

Queensland
Queensland Ballet Company,
129 Market Street, Brisbane 4000.
Tel (07) 229 3355.

Western Australia
West Australian Ballet Company,
825 Hay Street, Perth 6000.
Tel. (06) 321 5979.

Tasmania
Tasmanian Dance Company,
197 Wellington Street, Launceston 7250.
Tel. (003) 31 6644.

DRAMA

It's easy to become involved in theatre in Australia. There are many youth theatre groups in each State and listed below is a selection of them. All of them offer the chance for eight to 25-year-olds to be trained as actors and to take part in stage productions. On top of this, experience in other areas, such as playwriting, directing, video-making, lighting and sound, music and theatre design are offered by some groups. These groups give you the opportunity to contribute to a production so that your interests and concerns can be expressed.

Experience in a youth theatre group is not only good fun, but can lead to greater things. In every State there are a number of professional theatre companies. Also, there are several tertiary courses in the dramatic arts, for example, those offered by the National Institute of Dramatic Art (NIDA) in Sydney. If you don't want a full-time career in the theatre, the many amateur companies would place lesser demands on your time and talents.

To join a youth theatre company there is usually no audition and no experience is needed. Most are free, though some have a small charge, so check first.

YOUTH THEATRE GROUPS

New South Wales
Australian Theatre for Young People,
3rd floor, 82-96 Myrtle Street,
Chippendale 2008.
Tel. (02) 698 7022.

Victoria
St Martins Youth Arts Centre,
St Martins Lane, South Yarra 3141.
Tel. (03) 267 2477.

South Australia
Carclew Youth Performing Arts Centre Inc.,
11 Jeffcott Street, North Adelaide 5006
Tel. (08) 267 5111.

Australian Capital Territory
Canberra Youth Theatre Company,
Gorman House, Batman Street,
Braddon 2601.
Tel. (062) 48 5057.

Queensland
Brisbane Youth Theatre,
Fairland Street, Mt Gravatt 4122.
Tel. (07) 369 2344.

Western Australia
The Playhouse Theatre-in-Education,
3 Pier Street, Perth 6000.
Tel. (09) 325 3344.

Tasmania
Salamanca Theatre Company,
79 Salamanca Place, Hobart 7000.
Tel. (002) 23 5259.

Bushrangers

Some bushrangers were bad for the image of the profession. Jack Bradshaw and "Lovely" Riley in 1876 held up and captured the bank manager of Coolah (N.S.W.). Unfortunately when they attempted to rob the bank, which was attached to the manager's residence, they were driven off by the midwife attending his pregnant wife.

Frank Gardiner was released from Darlinghurst gaol after serving ten years of a 32-year sentence. He was put on a ship for Hong Kong and eventually reached San Francisco where he ran a saloon called "The Twilight Star" under the alias of Frank "Smith", for the rest of his life.

At Thunderbolt's grave in the cemetery at Uralla (N.S.W.) there is a large memorial and a steel letter box for notes from visitors. The steel box is chained to the memorial to prevent it from being stolen by some modern-day bushranger.

The first gang of bushrangers was led by "Black Caesar", a West Indian negro who led a gang of "bolters" in the 1790s on the outskirts of Sydney. Eventually Governor Hunter offered a reward of 5 gallons of rum for his capture or death. A settler named Wimbow shot him dead.

Ned Kelly was first charged when he was 14. The offence was assaulting a Chinese with a stick. He spend nearly two weeks in prison but the charge was dismissed. Two other members of the Kelly Gang, Joe Byrne and Aaron Sherritt, were both imprisoned for six months for the same offence when they were young.

Kate Kelly, Ned's sister, was despised by her family for cashing in on her brother's life. She made stage appearances and claimed to have taken part in some of their activities. She died by drowning (thought to be suicide) at Forbes (N.S.W.) when still in her 30s.

The first bushrangers were convict "bolters" who had taken to the bush as a way of life marginally better than the convict settlement. When they were captured they received up to 1000

BUSHRANGERS

lashes and were returned immediately to the work gangs.

The bushranger Captain Moonlite, Andrew George Scott (1842–1880) was born in Ireland and was an Anglican preacher. Despite his religious background he killed a constable, and was executed.

If "Mad Dan" Morgan the infamous bushranger had lived in our times he would probably have been committed to a mental hospital. His fits of good humour and gentleness, alternating with uncontrollable rage, were classic symptoms of schizophrenia.

The bushranger Ben Hall (1838–1865) is generally regarded as the most gentlemanly of the bushrangers. As a wealthy young man he married Bridget Walsh who carried on a series of affairs with other men and eventually ran away with one of them. Ben Hall was wrongly accused of highway robbery and was acquitted, but he was bitter and turned to crime. Later he was betrayed by other bushrangers and killed near Forbes. He was mourned through the Forbes district as a man to be pitied rather than condemned.

Although it is believed that Dan Kelly the bushranger brother of Ned Kelly died at Glenrowan in 1880, for many years an old man who travelled Queensland with a push cart claimed that he was the infamous bushranger. To prove it he would show people the branded scar "Dan Kelly" on the inside of his thighs. He claimed that this was put there by his father with a poker as a punishment for burning Ned's ear with the poker. He had a great knowledge of the Kelly Gang's exploits and claimed that his wife had been killed by lightning. It is interesting that the body alleged to be Dan Kelly's was so badly burned that positive identification was not possible.

Martin Cash, around whom the television series *Cash and Co.* was based, was one of the few bushrangers to die of old age. He was transported from Ireland at the age of 18 for shooting a man in the backside while he was in a compromising situation with Cash's girlfriend. In 1836 he was working in the Hunter Valley and stealing cattle as a sideline. Two years later in Van Diemen's Land he was sentenced to seven years' gaol for theft, but escaped the same day. Over the next four years he was captured and escaped twice. During his arrest in 1843 he shot a constable dead, but his death sentence was commuted to 10 years on Norfolk Island. After his sentence he settled on a farm at Glenorchy, Tasmania.

The term "bushrangers" seems to be peculiarly Australian, having been used in the *Sydney Gazette* as early as 1805. It may have arisen from the comments of Sir Joseph Banks who said that the country could not be safe while convicts had permission "to range the country at large".

There was one bushranger with a difference—he was Chinese. Sam Poo was active in the Mudgee (N.S.W.) area and wounded a trooper at Coonabarabran. He was hunted down and captured in February 1865, tried for attempted murder and hanged.

Australians regard their bushrangers as folk heroes. To tell a person that he is as "game as Ned Kelly" is a great compliment.

"Thunderbolt" was a folk hero even before he died, but the story surrounding his death added to the

legend. He was being chased by a Constable Walker when the policeman shot his horse as he spurred it into the Rocky River. Thunderbolt turned to fight him, asking if he was married. When the constable said that he was, Thunderbolt said, "Remember your family". Walker called on him to surrender and he shouted "I'll die first", and tried to grapple with Walker, who shot him in the side. When he continued to attack him, Walker hit Thunderbolt over the head with a gun and he sank into the water. Walker pulled him out onto the river bank and decided that Thunderbolt was dead. He went to seek assistance but when they came back the bushranger had crawled into nearby scrub. He died soon after and only later did they find that his pistol was not loaded during the fight.

The bushranger "Captain" Melville was born Frank McCallum in Scotland. He was 16 when he was transported for seven years. In 1851, he crossed from Van Diemen's Land to Victoria, where he organised a gang, raiding homesteads in the Mount Macedon district. After capture he was sentenced to 32 years' hard labour. In 1856 he led an attempt to seize a launch but it was unsuccessful and a corporal was killed. He and the others involved were sentenced to death, but his sentence was commuted to life imprisonment. He was always troublesome and even his fellow convicts feared him and said that he was mad. He attacked warders, policemen and even the gaol Governor. When he was found dead in his cell a coroner's jury found that he had strangled himself with his own hands. No, I don't believe it either.

After Harry Power, Ned Kelly's mentor, was captured and sentenced to 15 years' hard labour in Pentridge gaol for his bushranging activities he survived the gaol sentence and was released in 1885. He took a job as an attendant aboard the convict hulk *Success* which had been converted into a convict museum and crowds flocked to his conducted tours. He enjoyed the notoriety of being the "oldest living bushranger". In 1891 while on holiday at Swan Hill he fell in the Murray River and drowned. A sad end for "the man who taught Ned Kelly".

Ned Kelly's body was buried in an unmarked grave in the condemned criminals section of the old Melbourne gaol, which means that it is now somewhere under the concrete floor of the police garage in Russell Street, Melbourne.

One of Captain Moonlite's gang, Gus Wernicke, was only just 15 when he died in a shoot-out with police near Wagga (N.S.W.) in 1879. He was less than 5 feet (150 centimetres) tall and died screaming from a bullet wound near the heart.

Bungling Jack Bradshaw had hardly any real succcess as a bushranger, being captured in just about every attempt at robbery, even minor theft. About 1905 he began to make a full-time career out of personal appearances in tent shows, lecturing, singing, dancing and writing books about his amazing (and mainly imaginary) bushranging experiences. He claimed to have met or ridden with every famous bushranger. He died comfortably in an old people's home in the 1930s, fully believing his own publicity that he was the "last of the notorious bushrangers".

The book and movie *The Chant of Jimmy Blacksmith* was based on the life of the Aboriginal bushranger, Jimmy Governor, who was hanged at Darlinghurst in January 1901.

Climate

NOT MUCH OF A CLIMATE

NO, BUT THERE'S PLENTY OF WEATHER

Australia is the world's driest continent and the rainfall that we have is extremely unreliable. The mean annual rainfall in Australia is 420 millimetres compared with a world mean of 660 millimetres. It has been estimated that 67 per cent of the rain that falls is lost in evaporation.

The highest and lowest temperatures on record for Australia's major cities are:

	Highest °C	Lowest °C
Sydney	45.3°	2.1°
Melbourne	45.6°	−2.8°
Canberra	42.2°	−10.0°
Brisbane	43.2°	2.3°
Adelaide	47.6°	0°
Perth	44.7°	1.2°
Hobart	40.8°	−2.8°
Darwin	40.5°	10.4°

The highest shade temperature ever recorded in Australia was 53.1°C (127.5°F). This was recorded at Cloncurry (Qld) in 1889.

The 1902 drought is regarded as Australia's worst drought year. Over 50 million sheep died.

The wettest place in continental Australia is Tully (Qld) with an annual average of 4554 millimetres (179.3 inches) of rainfall. The record for 24 hours is 907 millimetres (35.71 inches) at Crohamhurst (Qld) on 3 February 1893.

The driest place in Australia is Mulka (S.A.) with an annual average of 102.8 millimetres (4 inches).

The frostiest area of Australia is the New England Plateau around Armidale (N.S.W.). It has up to about 140 nights of frost yearly.

Northern Australia, like all tropical areas has only two seasons. It has a dry season, May to October, when little rain falls, and a wet season from January to March when heavy monsoonal rain occurs.

Marble Bar in north-western Western Australia has the hottest climate in Australia. In 1923–1924 Marble Bar recorded temperatures of 38°C (100°F) or more, for 160 consecutive days. Temperatures over 49°C (120°F) are quite common.

Creatures

The young of the platypus, who probably have enough problems already, are faced with the extra problem of a mother without nipples. The milk is secreted in glands beneath the skin and they drink by sucking at tufts of hair.

The teeth of wombats have no roots. They grow continually from a pulpy tissue on the gums.

Koalas do not live for long periods of time. It is thought that most of them do not live beyond 10 years. The greatest recorded age of a koala kept in captivity is 12 years.

Young sea lions may eventually grow to 3.6 metres (12 feet). They are born without the instinctive ability to swim and have to be taught by their mothers.

The first black swans were captured in Western Australia and exhibited in Europe by Willem de Vlamingh in 1697. Up until that time philosophers and scientists who wanted to give an example of something impossible or too preposterous for words, would use the black swan as an example.

The Australian kelpie is recognised as the world's best sheep dog. It has been bred from the border collie and the dingo.

There was an old belief that the fish caught in Australia's rivers carried on their bodies scenes of the places where they were caught.

Many people believe that the crocodile's skin is so thick that bullets will not penetrate it. In fact it is quite soft, but sometimes bullets strike the bony scutes which protrude close to the surface. Crocodiles are now protected species in Australia.

In common with many marsupials, the baby kangaroo is not born in its mother's pouch. After it is born it crawls through its mother's hair to get there. At this stage it is only 2.5 centimetres (an inch) long, and hairless. Once in the pouch it attaches itself to its mother's teat. In the early days many people believed that it was born through the teat.

A pademelon (or paddymelon) is not Irish nor is it a fruit. It is a small wallaby.

CREATURES

Cows cannot be milked by snakes despite some opinions to the contrary. There have been stories of cows being sucked dry by carpet snakes, but since the snakes can consume less than a litre of liquid their victims would have to be poor cows indeed, quite apart from the logistics of the situation.

It is a fact that once cane toads move into a locality the snakes seem to disappear. Old-timers believe that there is a peculiar odour emitted by the toads which is repulsive to snakes.

Early this century the whalemen of Eden on the southern coast of New South Wales used tame killer whales to round up sperm whales and force them into Twofold Bay, where they were killed from boats and taken ashore. The skeleton of "Old Tom", the most famous of the killer whales, is preserved in the museum at Eden.

Australia is the only country in the world with disease-free wild camels. They are exported to many parts of the world. The first camel was imported into Australia in 1840, but it was destroyed for causing the death of its owner. Large-scale importation started in 1860 when camels and their Afghan drivers were brought to Australia for the Burke and Wills expeditions.

Budgerigars, which have been bred in a variety of colours and are favourites as caged birds all over the world, originated from small green grass parrots native to inland Australia.

The Australian magpies are not the same species as the European magpies. Australian magpies are shrikes of the genus *Gymnorhina*, and are not really magpies at all.

Buffaloes are not native to Australia—they were introduced from Timor in 1825. They are hunted for their hides and meat but are regarded as disease spreaders and dangerous to Australia's cattle industry.

The dingo is not a true Australian native. Experts believe that it came to Australia with the Aborigines about 30,000 years ago.

The redback spider which is so much feared in rural Australia, particularly for its habit of nesting in toilets, is a close kin to America's black widow and New Zealand's katipo. Very few deaths have been recorded in Australia from their bites, but they do cause severe illness.

The largest lizard in Australia is the Perenty goanna which grows to a length of about 8 feet (2.4 metres).

In the northern regions termite mounds are described as magnetic because the long axis points north-south. Termites build them this way instinctively; the narrow end of the mound catches the least amount of sun at midday and receives the full sun only in early morning and late afternoon when it has least effect.

The emu is the biggest Australian bird, but the biggest bird that actually flies is the wedge-tailed eagle. Their wingspan can be over 2.1 metres (7 feet) wide and they live on rabbits, small wallabies and lizards. Despite tales to the contrary they seldom attack sheep or lambs.

The humble Australian yabbies or freshwater crayfish come in 82 different species. Some of the larger species are over 60 centimetres (2 feet) in length.

Sheep dogs show a natural inclination to either bring sheep towards the

handler, or to drive them away. Whichever tendency a puppy exhibits is used to make him into a "heading dog" to bring sheep in, or a "huntaway" to take them out. Some dogs will do both, but they are usually not good at heading.

Australia's crocodiles are now protected species. They have a bad reputation for killing people, but they are a lot less dangerous than we are. Since Australia was first settled they have killed a few of us, but we have probably killed a million of them in return. Who is deadlier?

Some people believe that snakes will not cross a rope, particularly if it is made of horsehair. They believe that if a rope is laid around a tent it will keep out the snakes. This is, of course, nonsense — snakes have been found coiled up asleep on ropes.

A surprisingly large number of people still believe the old story about "hoop snakes" which was used by old hands to frighten new settlers. The hoop snake was supposed to grab its tail in its mouth and roll along like a hoop. This is physically impossible.

The koala has an unusual feature for an arboreal creature — it has no tail. Zoologists believe that this indicates that at one stage of its evolution it lived on the ground. It is more or less a type of wombat that took to the trees.

The thylacine or marsupial wolf may be extinct. It is over 50 years since there was a definite sighting, although naturalists hope that some still remain in south-western Tasmania. They existed in large numbers when white settlers first started farming in Tasmania and were the victims of a deliberate eradication campaign.

Australia's flying foxes or fruit-bats live in colonies of up to 50,000. At night they fly for kilometres searching for fruit and nectar. In New South Wales and Queensland they sometimes cause great damage to domestic fruit trees.

The dingo is closely related to the ordinary dog but there are certain differences. Its ears are constantly erect, it has a brushy tail and its own particular gait, and yelps rather than barking. It also smells quite different (even from a distance).

Sharks, unlike the bony fishes, do not have an air or swim bladder to keep them afloat. As a result sharks must swim continuously to avoid sinking to the bottom.

Tasmania has a much wider range of small wallabies and pademelons than the mainland States, mainly because foxes have never been introduced into Tasmania. Naturalists believe that foxes and feral cats have been responsible for the elimination of dozens of species of small marsupials.

The honey possum of south-western Australia is a highly specialised mammal. It has a beak-like snout and a slim, darting brush-tipped tongue which allows it to feed on the nectar in wildflowers.

Koalas have cheek pouches on the inside of their faces which help in the chewing and digestion of bulky leaf foods.

Although living marsupials are found only in Australia and South America, fossils of marsupials have been found all over the world. This is why marsupials are sometimes referred to as living fossils.

CREATURES

Australian tortoises have a special characteristic. Instead of pulling their heads into the shell like other species they fold them sideways around the shell.

Some species of Australian frogs survive in dry weather by filling themselves up with water and burying themselves in the ground. They can survive in this way from one wet season to the next.

The galah was a favourite bird of the early settlers, who claimed that it made the best parrot pie.

Baby crimson rosellas are not the brilliant crimson colour of their parents. Until their third year they are green.

The kookaburra is the biggest kingfisher in the world but unlike all other kingfishers it rarely eats fish. It lives on snakes, small animals and the young of other birds.

White ants are not ants and they are not particularly white either. They are termites, related to cockroaches rather than the ants. They are blind and are a yellowish colour.

Apart from man, the longest-living mammal in Australia is probably the killer whale *Orcinus orca*. "Old Tom" who assisted the whalers at Eden (N.S.W.) made regular visits from 1843 to 1930; which is a period of 87 years.

Earwigs can look very frightening when they raise their pincers in the air, particularly the Grant earwig at 5 centimetres (2 inches) long. However, although they can pinch they have no sting. In the past people believed that they would crawl in your ear given a chance, hence the name, but there is no truth in that. They are unusual for insects because the females protect their eggs and mother their young like chickens.

The bustard or wild turkey is reputed to be Australia's most edible wildlife. It has been hunted almost to extinction, but specimens caught have been weighed at 14 kilograms (32 pounds).

The largest shark found in Australian waters is the basking shark which may grow up to 13 metres (45 feet). White pointers of over 10 metres (35 feet) are quite common.

Australia's largest freshwater fish is the Murray cod. The biggest one caught weighed 113 kilograms (250 pounds) and was over 1.8 metres (6 feet) long.

When Australia was first settled there were three species of emu — the mainland emu, the King Island emu, and the Kangaroo Island emu. Both the latter became extinct in the early days of settlement.

The Australian terrier was bred in Australia during the 1860s from the combination of Scotch terriers and Dandie Dinmont terriers. When they were first bred they were referred to as "broken-coated terriers". The breed has become quite popular in England this century and has been crossbred with Yorkshire and Irish terriers.

That delicious fish, the barramundi, has peculiar habits. The male fish carries the eggs in its mouth until they hatch.

The bellbird or bell-miner found in eastern Australia is a small olive-green bird with distinctive eye patches and a tinkling call. Some hard-to-please people refer to it as the headache bird,

CREATURES

because they claim that the repetitious chiming sound gives them a headache.

The noisy cicadas which make such a racket on warm evenings may be up to 20 years old when they die. The female cicada lays eggs in slits cut in the limbs of trees. When they hatch, the young crawl down the tree and burrow into the roots where they suck sap. It is believed that they may spend anything up to 20 years in the ground. Then, when almost mature they climb back up the tree and after a final moult emerge in a winged form. In this adult form they usually live only a few days.

The deadly bluebottle or Portuguese man-of-war is not the single creature it appears to be but a collection of creatures all born from a single egg but performing specialised functions. Reproduction, food catching, digestion and so on are all carried out by separate creatures within the colony.

The Argentine ant was first found in Melbourne in 1931 and has since spread through the whole country. It is a serious pest because it destroys domestic species of ants and other insects. It also cultivates aphis colonies on plants to "milk" them and this can destroy crops. It attacks domestic pantries and industrial stores and will eat virtually anything that is edible. It is extremely difficult to control.

The emu is not only Australia's biggest bird, it is the second biggest bird in the world (after the ostrich), growing to 150 centimetres (5 feet). One thing not often appreciated is that it is an excellent swimmer if forced to take to the water.

The biggest Australian spider is *Selenotypus plunipes* which lives in central Australia. Specimens have been found up to 24 centimetres (9.5 inches) across including its legs.

Australia's bush fly problem is world famous. The problem is that they breed in tremendous numbers in the dung of cattle, which are not part of the local ecology. Cattle drop an average of more than 10 pads of dung a day, and there are over 30 million cattle in Australia—that is 300 million pads a day. In the time that it has taken you to read this paragraph about another 200,000 have been dropped. The answer to the problem is now thought to be in finding a species of dung beetle which will break up the pads without disturbing the ecology in some undesirable way.

The now extinct grand wombat-like marsupial, diprotodon, died out about 13,000 B.C. It was still around when the Aborigines first arrived in Australia.

In the early days emus were hunted and rendered down for their oil. Emu oil was used as a treatment for rheumatism, to cure the bruises and sprains of horses and bullocks, to soften the leather of saddles and for oiling guns.

The early explorers do not seem to have been particularly attached to their horses. "Billy", Robert O'Hara Burke's horse, carried the explorer from Melbourne to the Gulf of Carpentaria and halfway back again. He was killed for food and eaten by the explorer without any comment other than that the flesh was "healthy and tender but without a trace of fat".

Rabbits were introduced to Australia in 1866 by Thomas Austin of Barwon Park near Geelong. He released a few to provide sport for himself and his guests. By the 1880s over a million hectares

CREATURES

(2.5 million acres) had been made useless because of them. When a prize was offered for a successful way of destroying them the great Louis Pasteur suggested chicken cholera, but this was ignored. There is a story about a farmer who went to town for a week to buy a reaper and binder to harvest his crop. When he returned the rabbits had eaten the lot.

Most horses have done very well if they live to 20 years of age. "Monty", a light draught horse from Albury (N.S.W.) lived to be over 52 years old. He was born in 1917 and died in 1970.

Australia has over 70 species of scorpions and some of them have a poison sting which is very painful. They are related to spiders and ticks (arachnids), live mainly on insects and are primarily nocturnal in habit. The biggest Australian scorpions are about 10 centimetres (4 inches) long. Scorpion stings are rarely fatal.

The wattle-birds are large species of honeyeaters. Their name has nothing to do with wattle trees, but refers to the fleshy appendages, wattles, that hang from their necks similar to those on chickens.

GESTATION PERIODS OF POPULAR MAMMALS AND PETS

AUSTRALIAN MAMMALS

Platypus (*Ornithorhynchus anatinus*) • 10–12 days
Echidna (*Tachyglossus aculeatus*) • 14 days
Spotted-tailed Quoll (*Dasyurus maculatus*) • 21 days
Kowari (*Dasyuroides byrnei*) • 30–35 days
Tasmanian Devil (*Sarcophilus harrisii*) • 31 days
Northern Brown Bandicoot (*Isoodon macrourus*) • 12 days
Koala (*Phascolarctos cinereus*) • 31 days
Wombat (*Vombatus ursinus*) • Unknown
Sugar Glider (*Petaurus breviceps*) • 20 days
Mountain Brushtail Possum (*Trichosurus caninus*) • 15–17 days
Yellow-footed Rock-wallaby (*Petrogale xanthopus*) • 31 days
Tasmanian Pademelon (*Thylogale billardierii*) • 30 days
Whiptail Wallaby (*Macropus parryi*) • 34–38 days
Eastern Grey Kangaroo (*Macropus giganteus*) • 36 days
Wallaroo (*Macropus robustus*) • 32 days

OTHER COMMON MAMMALS

Cat (*Felis catus*) • 63 days
Dog (*Canis familiaris*) • 61 days
Rat (*Rattus rattus*) • 22 days
Pig (*Sus scrofa domestica*) • 110–120 days
Hippopotamus (*Hippopotamus amphibius*) • 240 days
Blue Whale (*Sibbaldus musculus*) • 330 days
Horse (*Equus caballus*) • 320–355 days
Monkey (*Macacus rhesus*) • 146–180 days
Mouse (*Mus musculus*) • 21 days
Guinea pig (*Cavia porcellus*) • 63–75 days

Rodents are the most prolific breeders amongst mammals. A house mouse or a brown rat can regularly produce 10 or more young every three weeks under ideal conditions, and a young rodent may begin breeding at about two months old. The rabbit would be lucky to rear eight young every eight weeks.

Disasters

AUSTRALIA'S FLATTEST PAVLOVA: DARWIN 1974

We hear much of the ships wrecked on the Australian coast in the early days but there was a great impact on Australia when the clipper *Royal Charter* was wrecked in Moelfre Bay, Wales, in 1859. Among the 459 people drowned were many miners who were returning home after making fortunes on the Victorian goldfields, and many pillars of Australian society.

Australia's worst building fire killed 30 elderly men at the William Booth Memorial Home in Melbourne in August 1966. The building was full of sleeping cubicles separated only by plywood partitions, and a fire was started in one of them by an overturned radiator.

In 1910 the Blue Anchor liner *Waratah* of 16,800 tons was making its second voyage back to England from Australia. Between Durban and Cape Town in South Africa it completely disappeared with its 380 passengers on board. No trace of them was ever found.

In the last 200 years there have been over 6000 ships wrecked in Australian waters. Shipwrecks were very common in the early part of last century because of the lack of accurate maps and charts. However, the experiences of one group of people in 1829 were remarkable even for those days. A group of people left Sydney for Raffles Bay, near what is now Darwin, aboard the colonial cutter, *Mermaid*. On entering Torres Strait the boat ran ashore and was lost, but all on board were able to scramble on to the rocks. Three days later they were picked up by the *Swiftsure* from Tasmania. Another three days later it also ran ashore and was wrecked. All were saved by another Tasmanian vessel, the *Governor Ready*. Unbelievably, before it made Raffles Bay the *Governor Ready* was also wrecked, but all of the people from the *Mermaid*, the *Swiftsure* and the *Governor Ready* managed to save themselves in the long boats. Sure enough all were rescued, this time by

DISASTERS

the *Comet*. Almost inevitably, it seems, the *Comet* was also wrecked, again without loss of life. This time they were all picked up by another Tasmanian vessel, the *Jupiter*. The *Jupiter* made it to Raffles Bay, but as it was entering the harbour it also ran ashore and was badly damaged. A few months later the Raffles Bay settlement was abandoned and they would all have had to sail back to Sydney.

The greatest shipping disaster in Australian history was probably the wreck of the schooner *Cataraqui* in 1845. Travelling from Liverpool in England to Melbourne, it was wrecked on the coast of King Island. Four hundred and six of the passengers and crew died. The disaster led to the building of the Cape Otway lighthouse in Victoria to show ships the point at which to make for the coast.

When the *Cataraqui* was wrecked, among the victims were 38 residents of the village of Tackley in England. When Phillip Derriman from Sydney visited the village in 1978 he found that no news of the disaster had ever reached the village. A vellum scroll to commemorate the lost victims has now been placed in the local church — 135 years later.

The worst flood in Australian history occurred in 1852 at Gundagai when the Murrumbidgee broke its banks at about midnight on 23 June. Whole families perished, houses collapsed and survivors were marooned on rooftops. Hundreds were left clinging to trees for days before being rescued. The death toll is uncertain but the town was almost completely destroyed, and 89 bodies were recovered.

One of Australia's worst rail disasters happened at Sunshine station (Vic.) in 1908. Easter holiday makers were returning from Ballarat and Bendigo to Melbourne when the Bendigo train ran into the back of the train from Ballarat. Forty-four people were killed and 430 were injured.

The most damaging earthquake ever in Australia occurred in Western Australia in 1968. There was substantial damage in Perth and Kalgoorlie, and the town of Meckering was completely demolished.

Black Friday, 13 January 1939, when 71 people died in bushfires was the worst bushfire day on record until Ash Wednesday, 16 February 1983, which exceeded it in the extent of death and destruction of property.

Australia's first major air disaster occurred in 1931, only 15 months after Kingsford Smith and Ulm formed Australian National Airways Ltd. The *Southern Cloud* disappeared in bad weather on a Sydney-Melbourne flight, with eight passengers and crew. The remains of the plane and its passengers were not found until 1958, near the Victoria-New South Wales border. It was about 25 kilometres (15 miles) off course.

Cyclone Tracy which wrecked Darwin in 1974 had a forerunner which was much worse. In 1889 Cyclone Mahina struck the north Queensland coast wrecking 100 boats and killing over 400 people. A tidal wave over 15 metres (50 feet) high broke over the shore and went up to 5 kilometres (3 miles) inland.

Australia's worst mine disaster occurred at Port Kembla in 1902. Two hundred and seventy-eight miners were trapped underground and only 182 were rescued. Some of the bodies of the 96 miners lost were never recovered.

DISASTERS

Australia's worst influenza epidemic was experienced in the winter of 1918. Most of the victims were adults in the prime of their lives, between 20 and 40 years of age. It is estimated that 10,000 people died in about eight months.

Beneath the Westgate Bridge at Williamstown (Vic.) there is a memorial to the 35 workers who were killed when part of it collapsed during construction. The collapse on 15 October 1970 set the construction back about five years and increased the cost by four times the original estimate.

The biggest bushfire ever in Australia burned out 2.5 million hectares (6 million acres) in the Barkly Tableland of the Northern Territory in June 1974. This compares with a maximum of 0.5 million hectares (1 million acres) in any fire in Victoria or South-eastern Australia.

In 1964, the Australian aircraft-carrier *Melbourne* made its first kill: its companion vessel, the destroyer *Voyager*. Eighty-two of the *Voyager*'s crew died when the *Melbourne* cut it in half. Then in 1969 the *Melbourne* did it again—the American destroyer *Frank E. Evans* was the victim this time and 74 of its crew died. Inquiries cleared the *Melbourne* in both incidents but the vessel established a reputation for being accident-prone as planes were lost and even fell into the sea from its deck.

When the ore-carrier S.S. *Lake Illawarra* struck the Tasman Bridge across the River Derwent in Hobart in 1975, two piers and three spans of the bridge collapsed, sinking the ship. Seven crewmen on the ship and at least four people in motor cars were killed. The ore-carrier remains where it sank.

On 6 February 1938 three huge waves washed 300 swimmers off a sandbank and scoured away the sandbank itself, at Bondi beach in Sydney. About 70 lifesavers of the Bondi Surf Club rescued them and 42 were unconscious when brought back to the beach. Four of those died and the body of a fifth victim was washed up later. The day is sometimes referred to as Black Sunday.

When Cyclone Tracy struck Darwin on Christmas Day 1974 the city was wrecked. Winds reached up to 217 kilometres per hour (135 miles per hour) and over 50 people were killed. Ninety per cent of the buildings in the city were damaged or destroyed—a damage bill of over $50 million.

Australia's worst rail disaster occurred at Granville, Sydney, on 18 January 1977. The train from the Blue Mountains, packed with commuters, jumped the tracks just before the Bold Street bridge and knocked down the bridge stanchion, causing it to collapse onto the train. Eighty people were killed and 83 injured (some of whom died subsequently). It took 31 hours to remove the last bodies from the wreckage.

In a busy harbour you can expect ships to sometimes be in the wrong place at the wrong time, particularly ferries which cross shipping lanes. However, the only major disaster on Sydney Harbour was the sinking of the ferry *Greycliffe* in November 1927. She was run down by the steamer *Tahiti* and sank. The death toll was 40, which included many children on their way home from school.

Events

January 26 was not the date of the landing of the First Fleet at Botany Bay. The landing at Botany Bay was on 20 January 1788. The move to Sydney Cove, and the beginning of the first permanent settlement, was six days later.

Australia Day was first celebrated as Anniversary Day on 26 January 1818, the 30th anniversary of the arrival of the First Fleet at Sydney Cove. It was later referred to as Foundation Day. The name Australia Day was first adopted in Victoria in 1931.

The first Commonwealth Parliament met in the Melbourne Exhibition Buildings on 29 April 1901. It did not meet in Canberra until 9 May 1927.

Katherine (N.T.) which is 345 kilometres (220 miles) inland from Darwin has its own Carnival in June each year with a parade, comedy water sports, a craft exhibition, historical tours, and sports. If you are not a great athlete you may have a chance to become a champion anyway as one of the major events at the Katherine Carnival is the beef-eating championship of Australia.

All States except Western Australia celebrate the Queen's birthday by taking the nearest Monday as the Queen's birthday holiday. The long weekend is an occasion for setting off fireworks.

For many years Sydney held a Waratah Spring Festival each year, but it finished in 1974 due to lack of public interest. However, somebody must have missed it because in January, 1977 the first Festival of Sydney was held. The festival starts with an open-air concert and fireworks display on New Year's Eve and lasts for the whole of January. It has events for everyone including yachting regattas, the Great Ferry Boat Race, a children's film festival, concerts and exhibitions.

Cunnamulla-Eulo (Qld) has its own festival each year, in August. It is an opal mining area and most activities are centred around fossicking for gem-stones. The highlight, though, is the annual sports meeting with prizes for such events as log-tossing, lizard racing, and catching the greasy pig.

The Adelaide Festival of Arts is much more cultural than most Australian festivals. It is held every second year in March and features opera, ballet, orchestral and choral concerts, chamber music, plays, recitals, jazz, youth activities and rock concerts. Leading cultural figures from all over the world attend and it is recognised as one of the world's leading cultural events.

Although Alice Springs (N.T.) is in one of Australia's lowest rainfall areas, and the Todd River there seldom has any water in it, this does not stop the residents from holding a regatta every year. Henley-on-Todd is held every August in the dry river bed. The "yachtsmen" and "yachtswomen" have bottomless boats so that they can stand inside them and run, carrying the "boats". In the same week the Camel Cup is held with up to 20 camels competing in the final. There is never a dull moment in the "Alice" because they also have the Bangtail Muster in May with humorous floats, sports and entertainment. Then in November there is the Folklorico Festival of foods, music, crafts and cultures from other countries.

Commonwealth Day was formerly called Empire Day and was celebrated on 24 May, Queen Victoria's birthday. It is now celebrated throughout the British Commonwealth on 11 June which is the official birthday of the Queen. It is not a public holiday in Australia.

Korumburra (Vic.) must be the only place in the world with a festival in honour of a worm. The Karmai Festival, held each year in March is named after the giant Gippsland worm, which the Aborigines called "karmai". A feature of the festival is the parade led by a gigantic pink plastic worm carried by dozens of local schoolchildren.

Nearly all of the major towns and cities of Australia have their own local festivals or carnivals. Among the many are:

Albany (W.A.) • Mardi Gras every March
Ballarat (Vic) • Begonia Festival each March
Barossa Valley (S.A.) • Vintage Festival in odd-numbered years, over the Easter Holidays
Bendigo (Vic) • Easter Fair each Easter
Bowral (N.S.W.) • Tulip Time every November
Derby (W.A.) • Boab Festival in June and July every year
Geelong (Vic) • Floral festivals in March and October
Goulburn (N.S.W.) • Lilac City Festival in October each year
Grafton (N.S.W.) • Jacaranda Festival every November
Gympie (Qld) • Gold Rush festival in October
Mt Gambier (S.A.) • International Bavarian Festival in January
Mt Isa (Qld) • Rotary Rodeo every August
Orange (N.S.W.) • Apple Country Fair in March
Townsville (Qld) • Townsville-Pacific Festival every June
Tumut (N.S.W.) • Falling Leaf Festival every April
Wyndham (W.A.) • Top of the West Festival in August
Young (N.S.W.) • Cherry Festival every November

Although John Batman is regarded as one of the founders of Melbourne, the John Batman Festival is held in Launceston (Tas.) in March each year. Batman lived in the Launceston area before he sailed across to Port Phillip Bay in 1835 and is regarded more as a hero in Northern Tasmania than he is in Victoria.

EVENTS

Melbourne's Moomba Festival held every Autumn in late February and early March, is a festival of fun, entertainment, sport and culture. It has Australia's biggest parade which passes through the centre of the city. The parade is held on the last day of the festival, which is the Labour Day public holiday. So great has been the impact of Moomba that many people believe that the holiday is a Moomba Day holiday.

One of Australia's quaintest festivals is the annual "schuetzenfest" or shooting festival held at Hahndorf (S.A.) in the Adelaide hills. This area was settled last century by German settlers and they have maintained many of the traditions of old Germany, including the schuetzenfest. There are exhibitions, historical re-enactments, displays, shooting contests and lots of beer drinking.

The Tasmanian Fiesta is held over the Christmas-New Year period. It is a statewide festival which coincides with the finish of Australia's two major ocean yacht races, the Sydney to Hobart yacht race, and the Westcoaster from Melbourne to Hobart. There is a host of other sport, entertainment, and cultural events.

The Melbourne Cup is not just Australia's richest horse race, with prize money of over one million dollars. It is a public holiday for all people who live within 60 kilometres of Melbourne, and the whole country virtually comes to a standstill during the running of the race. In Melbourne it is the highlight of the social calendar. It is always held on the first Tuesday in November.

One of the most colourful and spectacular events each year is the Beer-can Regatta held in Darwin (N.T.) in mid-June. This is a series of boat races held on Darwin harbour using a tremendous variety of home-made craft constructed mainly out of empty beer cans. Some people spend months building the most elaborate craft in the shape of old sailing ships, Viking longships, ocean liners and other ships. Boats are raced in classes according to size. Other people spend many dedicated hours drinking the contents so that there is plenty of raw material for the boat builders to use.

The mining settlement of Tom Price in the Western Pilbara of Western Australia has a festival every year called the Tom Price Nameless Festival. There is a Nameless Beauty Queen, a road race, stalls, dancing, and a music hall. The name of the festival celebrates the fact that the settlement was originally nameless until it adopted its name from Thomas Moore Price, a vice-president of Kaiser Steel Ltd, who was largely responsible for the establishment of the mine.

Anzac Day is celebrated on 25 April every year in memory of Australians killed in all wars. The date was chosen because it was the anniversary of the landing of Australian troops at Gallipoli in Turkey on 25 April 1915. Although there was immense loss of life and the battle was a clear victory for the Turkish defenders it is regarded by many as the true birth of Australia as a nation.

Nobody really planned to start the Festival of Perth, but it started anyway. The University of Western Australia was teaching short courses and summer schools over its vacation period. It introduced plays and concerts to entertain the participants during the evenings. From this modest start grew one of Australia's major cultural events.

Fallacies

Modern research has contradicted the old belief that koalas never drink water. It is true that they seldom drink because of the condensation and rain water on the gum leaves that they eat is sufficient. But in dry weather, and particularly when they are ill, they do require water.

Australians like to regard themselves as great gamblers. In fact, per head of population Australia ranks well behind most European countries, several Asian countries and the U.S.A.

Shark attacks do not occur only in the warm Indian and Pacific oceans. In July 1983 swimmers at Bournemouth on the south coast of England were chased from the water by a giant thresher shark.

Govett's Leap in the Blue Mountains (N.S.W.) is not named for a bushranger who rode over the precipice rather than be captured. It was named after a government surveyor, William Romaine Govett, who discovered the spot in 1831. It makes a good story though.

The first merino sheep were not brought to Australia by John Macarthur. In 1797 Henry Waterhouse, a naval officer, brought the first of this ideal variety to New South Wales. He supplied lambs to many of the settlers, including Macarthur.

The first permanent settlers in Victoria were commonly believed to be the Henty Brothers who arrived at Portland in 1834. However there is strong evidence that the Mills brothers settled permanently at Port Fairy (then called Belfast) in 1826. Even at Portland the Hentys' claims have been firmly challenged by the Dutton family.

Ayers Rock is not the largest exposed rocky outcrop (monolith) in the world. This honour goes to Mount Augustus, near Carnarvon in Western Australia, which is twice the size of Ayers Rock.

Australia's first great operatic prima donna was not Dame Nellie Melba, but her mother Theodosia Stewart. Theodosia was the star of the first genuine operatic performance held in Australia which was at the Royal Victorian Theatre, Hobart, in 1842. She

FALLACIES

was brought from England for the season and afterwards remained in Australia.

Although he is regarded as Australia's greatest racehorse, Phar Lap was not bred in Australia. Like most of our great horses he was bred across the Tasman in New Zealand.

The author Nevil Shute (1899–1960) who among other things wrote *A Town Like Alice*, *No Highway* and *On the Beach*, was not an Australian. He was English and lived in Australia only in the last few years of his life.

Very few people are attacked by sharks anywhere in the world, including Australia. Far more people are killed by lightning than are killed by sharks.

Tiger sharks are not named for their fierceness or their attacks on swimmers. Their name arose from the prominent dark stripes on their backs and sides.

The highest point in Australian territory is not Mount Kosciusko. It is the volcanic peak Big Ben on Heard Island, which, at about 3000 metres (over 9000 feet) is about 600 metres (1800) feet higher than Mount Kosciusko.

It was a common belief among convicts in the first settlement that it was possible to walk to China if one could escape from the settlement. Many of those who escaped headed north with that in mind.

Pinchgut in Sydney Harbour did not get its name because it held convicts who starved on bread and water. It was called this by sailors referring to the narrowing of the harbour at that point.

The writer Henry Handel Richardson who wrote among other things, *The Getting of Wisdom*, was not a man. Her real name was Ethel Henrietta Richardson. She had to use a male pen-name to receive serious recognition as a writer.

Despite our fond belief that we are one of the world's great sporting nations and that we perform best in the world at the Olympics considering our population, this is, unfortunately, not true. Countries which have a higher ratio of Olympic Games medals to population than Australia include Sweden (three times our ratio), Denmark, Switzerland and East Germany.

Koalas are often wrongly referred to as koala bears or native bears. They are in no way related to bears.

Olivia Newton-John is not really an Australian. She was born in England and lived in Australia for only a few years.

The Bee-Gees (Gibb brothers), are not Australians. They were born in England and still regard it as their home. They only lived for a short while in Australia and were never Australian citizens.

Australia is not the only country where voting in elections is compulsory. Among other countries where it is compulsory are Belgium, Austria and the Netherlands.

Australia is generally regarded as the world's biggest island. However, Afro-Eurasia is also an island, and so are the Americas and Antarctica, all bigger than Australia.

There is nothing new in the slogan "Advance Australia". It was the masthead of the *Sydney Gazette* from 1824 onwards, and was later the slogan of the Victoria Land League in their

campaign to have the squatters' landholdings distributed to small holders in 1856.

Although Charles Darwin visited Australia in 1836, he never visited the area which carries his name. He toured the Blue Mountains-Bathurst area (N.S.W.) and Van Diemen's Land but did not visit northern Australia.

Despite the fact that there is more than one Alligator River in northern Australia, there are no alligators. Early settlers mistook the estuarine crocodiles and freshwater crocodiles for alligators because of their size. Alligators are, however, an entirely different genus.

The main road to Western Australia from the eastern states does not cross the Nullarbor Plain, except for about 30 kilometres (19 miles) on the eastern edge. So those "We crossed the Nullarbor" stickers are something of an exaggeration.

The great advertising gimmick for General Motors-Holden when the first Holdens were produced in the late 1940s, was that this was "Australia's own car". However, the car was designed and planned in the United States and the first true Australian Holden did not appear until 1961. Another fallacy is that the Americans put in a lot of capital to start the company—in fact all of the money came from Australian sources with guarantees from the Australian Government; no capital came from American sources.

Gold was not first discovered in Australia by Edward Hargraves. The first official recorded gold discovery was at Bathurst (N.S.W.) in 1823, by James McBrien, a surveyor. As early as 1816 a convict was punished for possession of gold in the same area. Hargraves received the credit and reward for discovery of gold at Ophir (N.S.W.) in 1851. Even then it was his partners who discovered it while he was away in Sydney.

"Two-up", the old Australian gambling game is not Australian at all. It was an old English game called "pitch and toss". It is also sometimes called "swy" after the German word "zwei" meaning two.

The rock adder is not a snake but a broad-tailed rock gecko, which is a harmless lizard with small legs. It is often found in the sandstone areas around Sydney.

Despite Jack Moses' poem "Nine Miles from Gundagai" the dog on the tuckerbox does not sit there 9 miles from Gundagai—it is about 5 miles.

Firsts

The world's first ice-making works was established in Geelong (Vic.) by James Harrison, in 1851. Prior to that time ice could be obtained only by cutting it in blocks from frozen lakes in the mountains.

The world's first meat-freezing works was started by Thomas Mort, in Sydney, in 1879. His first cargo of meat to London, which consisted of 41 tonnes of beef and mutton, arrived in excellent condition.

The first solo flight from Britain to Australia was made by Bert Hinkler in 1928. After breaking and setting many other solo aviation records, he was killed in 1938 when he crashed near Florence, Italy, while trying to break the speed record for a Britain to Australia flight.

The Australian Flying Doctor Service, founded in 1928, was the first of its kind anywhere in the world.

The "Harvester Judgment" of 1907 established the principle of a basic wage for Australian workers. It was the first such nationwide minimum wage to be set anywhere in the world.

INVENTION OF SPEEDO RASH

The first European residents of Australia were probably the two mutinous crew members of the Dutch ship *Batavia* who were abandoned near Champion Bay (W.A.) in October, 1629.

The first point on the Australian mainland sighted by Cook's expedition was Point Hicks on the south-eastern coast of Victoria.

The first clergyman in Australia was Richard Johnson (1753–1827) who came with the First Fleet as chaplain. He built the first church in Sydney (and Australia) at his own expense and started the first schools.

The first man to be executed in New South Wales was Thomas Barrett. He was convicted of stealing stores and hanged in 1788.

The Australian William Farrer (1845–1906) was the first person to breed rust-free varieties of wheat. Before that rust fungus made it difficult to grow wheat in areas where rainfall exceeded 508 millimetres (20 inches) per year.

Australia's first university was the University of Sydney founded in 1850.

The first discovery of coal in Australia was made in 1797 by Lieutenant John Shortland who found it near Newcastle while searching for escaped convicts.

In 1944 the Australian Government became the first to introduce "Pay as you earn" income tax.

The first theatrical performance in Australia was George Farquhar's play *The Recruiting Officer*. It was performed by a cast of convicts in Sydney on 4 June 1789 in a mud hut. In 1796 an amateur theatre commenced under Robert Sidaway, a former convict, but it was closed down by the authorities after it was discovered that thieves were checking on who was attending, then robbing their houses.

Not surprisingly, the first book printed in Australia was a military manual. It was the *New South Wales General Standing Orders*, published by George Howe in 1802. The name of the first novel to be published in Australia is open to question but it seems to have been *Quintus Servinton* by Henry Savery, published in 1831 in Hobart.

Australia's first newspaper was the *Sydney Gazette* published by the government printer, George Howe, on 5 March 1803.

The first bushranger was reputed to be Michael Howe, an English highwayman transported to Van Diemen's Land in 1812. He was killed in 1818 after terrorising settlements throughout the colony. Howe referred to himself as "Governor of the Rangers".

The first opera written, composed and produced in Australia was Isaac Nathan's *Don John of Austria* (1847). Nathan had been a successful composer in England, but fled to Australia to escape his creditors. He claimed to be descended from the King of Poland and it was believed that he was a spy for the English royal family in European courts. He was the first man to be killed by a Sydney tram, in 1864.

The first team of Australian cricketers to play in England was made up entirely of Aborigines. The team went to England in 1868. They played 43 matches, winning 14, drawing 15 and losing 14. When they returned to Australia only two of them continued to play cricket.

The first Australian Rules match was played between Scotch College and Melbourne Grammar School in August 1858 which was eight years before the first organised game of soccer in England, at Battersea on 31 March 1866. The goal posts were 1.5 kilometres (nearly 1 mile) apart and 40 players per side took three afternoons to reach a decision.

Bondi Surf Club was the first to use the surf rescue reel. The first person ever rescued using the reel was a 14-year-old schoolboy called Charles Kingsford Smith, whose later glorious career made him a fitting subject for this singular honour.

Australia's first strike by free labourers was in 1824 when the colony's coopers went on strike for higher wages. They were unsuccessful, despite believing that they had the Governor over a barrel.

The first governor-general of Australia was the Earl of Hopetoun who took office at Federation in 1901, but the

FIRSTS

first Australian-born governor-general was Sir Isaac Isaacs who took office in 1931. When Sir Isaac was appointed many people believed that the fact that he was an Australian made it unconstitutional. A petition with 130,000 Australian signatories who described themselves as "empire loyalists" was sent to the King, but Isaacs was still appointed.

It used to be said that England had the first postage stamps, but pre-paid postage began in New South Wales in November 1838, two years before it began in England. It consisted of writing paper embossed with a 1½d. stamp, about the size of a 20 cent piece.

The first adhesive Australian postage stamp to be issued was the New South Wales one penny crimson-lake-coloured "Sydney Views". It was first issued on 1 January 1850. The States continued to issue their own stamps until the first Commonwealth issue in 1913 which was the kangaroo issue in ten denominations.

The first road constructed in Australia was built in September 1788 from the centre of the first settlement to the rock crusher at Dawes Point. The first main road was from Sydney to Rose Hill (Parramatta), opened in 1794.

The first boat built in Australia was *The Rose Hill Packet*. This 10 ton vessel was worked by sails and oars and was launched in October 1789. It was used to transport goods between Rose Hill (Parramatta) and Circular Quay.

The first motor car built in Australia was built by Herbert Thomson of Melbourne in 1898. It was a steam-driven phaeton of five horsepower, with pneumatic tyres, and it created confusion and excitement wherever it was driven.

Australia's first motor races were held on the old racecourse at Aspendale, Victoria in 1904. The first Australian Grand Prix took place on a dirt track at Phillip Island (Vic.) in 1928.

Australia's first unpowered lighter-than-air vehicle was that used by William Dean in Melbourne in February 1858. The craft known as the *Australasian* used coal gas and floated for 11 kilometres (7 miles) across Melbourne.

Secret ballots for elections were an Australian idea and were first introduced in Victoria and South Australia in 1856, in New South Wales and Tasmania in 1858, Queensland in 1859 and in Western Australia in 1878. Where a secret ballot is used overseas it is sometimes called the "Australian ballot".

Australia's first telephone was installed at Yanga homestead, near Balranald (N.S.W.) This was probably because its owner, James Comyn was a nephew of Alexander Graham Bell, the inventor.

The tradition of throwing streamers at and from departing ships originated in Sydney. In 1909 the son of a newsagent, Arthur Thomas, cut up strips of coloured wallpaper to sell on the wharves. The practice soon spread to other cities.

Australia was the first country to conduct rainmaking experiments with any success. The first successful experiment was at Bathurst in 1947 which was made by "seeding" clouds with silver iodide crystals.

Australia's first gold record (the only Australian gold "78") was Slim Dusty's record of "The Pub with no Beer".

Geography

Today I shall create Australia!

Don't leave Tasmania off. They're very sensitive.

Australia lies between the east longitudes 113° 9' and 153° 39' and between latitudes 10° 41' and 43° 29'. Nearly 40 per cent of its area is north of the Tropic of Capricorn.

Australia's area is 7,682,300 square kilometres (2,966,151 square miles), which is slightly smaller than the mainland United States (without Alaska and Hawaii). It makes Australia the sixth largest country in the world after the U.S.S.R., Canada, China, U.S.A., and Brazil. It is half as big again as Europe without the Soviet Union.

Western Australia is by far the biggest State. It occupies just under a third of the Australian continent and has a coastline of about 7000 kilometres (4340 miles). It is 2414 kilometres (1500 miles) from north to south and 1609 kilometres (998 miles) from east to west. The Americans boast about the size of Alaska and the size of Texas, but Western Australia is bigger than the two of them put together.

The flat, desolate plateau which stretches over most of Western Australia, South Australia and the Northern Territory, is geologically one of the world's oldest areas.

In 1984 the populations of each State and Territory, largest first, were:
New South Wales • 5,406,950
Victoria • 4,075,540
Queensland • 2,505,270
Western Australia • 1,382,470
South Australia • 1,352,910
Tasmania • 437,260
Australian Capital Territory • 244,470
Northern Territory • 138,780

The biggest cities and their 1984 populations are, in order of size:
Sydney • 3,355,250
Melbourne • 2,864,600
Brisbane • 1,138,400
Adelaide • 969,200
Perth • 969,100
Newcastle • 414,700
Wollongong • 235,000
Canberra • 255,900
Gold Coast • 189,100
Hobart • 173,700
Geelong • 142,900

GEOGRAPHY

Darwin is the only capital which does not rate, with a population of 63,300.

Australia extends across three time zones. The eastern States, Queensland, New South Wales, Victoria and Tasmania and the Australian Capital Territory take their time from the 150°E longitude. South Australia and the Northern Territory take their time from the 142½°E longitude—that is, they are half an hour behind. Western Australia uses the 120°E longitude, and is two hours behind the eastern States. However in summer, Victoria, New South Wales and Tasmania have daylight saving while Western Australia does not, so there is a three hour difference.

Queensland occupies just under a quarter of Australia's area. It has 5207 kilometres (3328 miles) of coastline and land boundaries of 1625 kilometres (1007 miles). From north to south its greatest distance is 2092 kilometres (1297 miles) and from east to west 1448 kilometres (898 miles).

South Australia covers about one-eighth of the Australian continent. It has a coastline of 3540 milometres (2200 miles). It is about 1200 kilometres (744 miles) from east to west, 629 kilometres (390 miles) from north to south on the western side and 1324 kilometres (821 miles) at the eastern boundary.

New South Wales covers about one tenth of Australia's total area. Its coastline measures 1459 kilometres (905 miles). Its greatest width is 1216 kilometres (754 miles) and it is about 1100 kilometres (682 miles) from north to south.

Most westerly point on the Australian mainland is Steep Point in Western Australia.

The Northern Territory is bigger than all of the States except for Western Australia and Queensland. It is about 1600 kilometres (1000 miles) from north to south and 950 kilometres (580 miles) from east to west. The coastline is about 1650 kilometres (1030 miles) long.

Australia is only five per cent forest. This is not much when you consider that Canada is 35 per cent forest and Japan is 40 per cent forest.

Most northerly point in Australia is Sae Island in the Admiralty Islands, which is only 77 kilometres (48 miles) south of the equator.

The central point of mainland Australia is Central Mount Stuart, 844 metres (2770 feet) high and situated in the Northern Territory.

The southernmost point of Australia on the Tasmanian south coast is about the same distance from the equator as Cannes or Nice in the South of France or Toronto in Canada.

The most southerly point in any Australian territory is the South Pole (Australian Antarctic Territory) at 90°S.

The most easterly point of the Australian mainland is Cape Byron near Byron Bay in New South Wales. On the cape is Australia's most powerful lighthouse.

Australia's Antarctic territories have an area of 6.1 million square kilometres (2.4 million square miles). This is nearly as big as Australia itself.

The southernmost point of the Australian mainland is Wilson's Promontory in Victoria. Specifically, the most southerly point is imaginatively called South Point.

Victoria occupies one-34th of Australia's area. Its greatest length from west to east is 793 kilometres (492 miles) and its greatest breadth from north to south is 467 kilometres (290 miles). It has 1577 kilometres (978 miles) of coastline.

As things stand, Australia controls about half of Antarctica, subject to a treaty signed in 1959 and operative for 30 years from 1961 onwards. So the treaty is due for review in 1991 when some of the signatories—particularly Argentina, South Africa, the U.S.S.R. and the U.K. may not be willing to support Australia's continued control.

The difference between Australia and Australasia is that Australasia includes New Zealand and its dependencies. Sometimes the term Australasia is used to include all places south of the Wallace line, including New Guinea, but this usage of the term is less common.

Australia is the flattest continent with an average height above sea level of less than 300 metres (990 feet). This compares with a world-wide average of about 700 metres (2310 feet). Less than five per cent of Australia is above the 600 metre level (1980 feet).

Lake Eyre is the lowest spot in Australia. It is about 12 metres (40 feet) below sea level.

The Gulf of Carpentaria in the north of Australia is one of the world's shallowest large bodies of water. It is about the size of Tasmania and in no place is it deeper than 100 metres (330 feet). In much of its area it is no more than 2 metres (7 feet) deep. Consequently it is a marvellous habitat for prawns, which breed there in millions.

Off the coast of Kangaroo Island in South Australia there are deep submarine canyons where the depth has never been completely measured.

The Australian territory of Norfolk Island has no natural harbour. Anything brought to the island by sea has to be taken ashore in small boats. This has ceased to be a problem since the construction of the airstrip in 1947.

The Ashmore and Cartier Islands off the coast of the Northern Territory have been a territory of Australia since 1931. There are three islands with a total area of about 2.6 square kilometres (1 square mile). Their maximum height is about 2 metres (7 feet) and they are inhabited only by birds, hermit crabs, and the odd rat descended from the survivors of old shipwrecks.

Australia has a coastline of nearly 20,000 kilometres (12,400 miles). The coastlines of New South Wales and Victoria are almost the same length. Unusually, the Australian Capital Territory has a coastline. A small stretch of coast which is home to a naval base at Jervis Bay (N.S.W.) is part of the A.C.T.

The Darling River is Australia's longest. It rises in the Darling Downs of Queensland and flows south-westerly into the Murray near Wentworth (N.S.W.). Although it is nominally 2740 kilometres (1700 miles) long, for most of the year it is only a discontinuous chain of waterholes. It was named after Sir Ralph Darling, Governor of New South Wales from 1825 to 1831.

The highest mountain in Queensland is Mount Bartle Frere which is 1586 metres (5287 feet) above sea level. It was named after the President of the Royal Geographic Society in 1873, when it was discovered.

GEOGRAPHY

Although Lake Eyre is nominally the largest lake in Australia it seldom contains any water. It is usually a dry area covered by a salt crust up to 4.5 metres (15 feet) thick.

The largest natural freshwater lake in Australia is the Great Lake, Tasmania, which is 24 kilometres (15 miles) long, and between 4 and 9 kilometres (3 and 5 miles) wide.

The deepest place in an Australian lake is on the western side of Lake St Clair (Tas.) where the water is up to 200 metres (700 feet) deep.

The biggest bay on the Australian coastline is the Great Australian Bight, which has a coastline of over 1450 kilometres (900 miles). It goes from Cape Catastrophe (S.A.) to Cape Paisley (W.A.), a straight line distance of 1100 kilometres (690 miles).

Australia's highest waterfalls are the Wollomombi Falls which drop 481 metres (1580 feet) from the eastern edge of the New England Plateau (N.S.W.) The stream eventually runs into the Macleay River.

The biggest Australian caves are under the Nullarbor Plain. The Mullamullang Cave has more than 9 kilometres (6 miles) of passages. The deepest cave in Australia is the Khazad-Dum in Tasmania which is 310 metres (1020 feet) deep.

There are still many people who believe that there is oil beneath the Great Barrier Reef. Bores were sunk on Heron Island, Michaelmas Bay and Wreck Island in 1958–1959 but although base rock was found, hydrocarbons were negligible. However, there is nothing to protect the reef from further exploratory drilling.

Ball's Pyramid is an island close to Lord Howe Island, about 700 kilometres (434 miles) north-east of Sydney. It is a solid rock spire rising from a base of less than half a hectare (1¼ acres) (the size of five city blocks). Its spectacular spire is 564 metres (about 1800 feet) high. It was discovered and named by Lieutenant Ball in 1788.

Surely no other major world city is built on such a dirty, unimpressive river as the Yarra. It has been sneered at by people from all over the world with claims that it "flows upside down" or is "too thick to drink, too thin to plough". As early as 1886 Mark Kershaw wrote that it might make good hair oil. However, Melbourne's water supply, which is collected mainly at the headwaters of the Yarra, is acknowledged as the purest and best in the world.

Some of the water obtained from artesian bores in Queensland is believed to have been underground for thousands of years, and to have travelled for well over 1000 kilometres.

The Great Barrier Reef off Queensland's coast varies from between 16 kilometres (10 miles) and 240 kilometres (149 miles) in its distance from the coast. The reef area is really the sunken coastal plain which was once between the mountains and the old coastline, and is believed to have formed over about the last 30 million years.

One of the most interesting features of the Australian coastline is the Coorong, a landlocked stretch of water which runs parallel to Endeavour Bay in South Australia. It is over 130 kilometres (80 miles) long and from 1.5 to 5 kilometres (1 to 3 miles) wide and is a magnificent habitat for waterbirds. The Australian movie *Storm Boy* was filmed in the area.

GEOGRAPHY

Although Australia has no really high mountains, the Great Dividing Range is the fourth longest in the world after the Andes, the Rockies and the Himalayas–Karakoram–Hindu Kush.

Mount Elephant, the extinct volcanic cone in western Victoria, was used by swagmen as a landmark to keep themselves from getting lost. It can be seen for many kilometres on the flat plains and was referred to as the "swagman's lighthouse".

Ayers Rock is a granite monolith (or single rock) in the Northern Territory. It is 335 metres (1100 feet) high, 2.4 kilometres (1.5 miles) long and 1.6 kilometres (1 mile) wide. It measures 8 kilometres (5 miles) around the base. It is a sacred aboriginal site. The first European to visit it was the explorer William Gosse in 1873 who named it after the premier of South Australia at that time.

Tower Hill, the massive volcanic crater near Warrnambool (Vic.) must have been the site of an active volcano since the arrival of the Aborigines in Australia. Aboriginal artifacts have been found in the area, buried under a thick cover of volcanic ash.

The Murrumbidgee River at Wagga Wagga is hardly a major stretch of water, particularly in summer. However "Wagga beach" on the river is patrolled by members of the Wagga Surf Lifesaving Club.

The Northern Territory has a sparse population even by Australian standards. In a world where population density is often measured in hundreds per square kilometre, its population density is .07 per square kilometre, or seven people for every hundred square kilometres (40 square miles).

Lake George (N.S.W.) near Canberra is sometimes a lake 25 kilometres (15 miles) long and 10 kilometres (6 miles) wide, which is used for fishing and boating. At other times it has no water at all and is ploughed for crop-growing. The lake is an extinct volcanic crater and it is thought that a fissure beneath the surface opens and is then blocked by clay as the water drains away.

Mount Olga (N.T.) is a huge red conglomerate monolith 32 kilometres (20 miles) west of Ayers Rock. The Olgas cover 35 square kilometres (13 square miles) and are famous for the spectacular colours of the rocks which change with the position of the sun. The first European to sight them was Ernest Giles, who wanted to name them after his sponsor, the botanist Baron von Mueller. However von Mueller persuaded him to name them after Queen Olga of Spain.

Health

There are still leper colonies in many parts of the world, including some leprosariums in northern Australia, most notably near Palm Island off the Queensland coast.

It was Dame Kate Isabel Campbell, an Australian doctor, who first identified the cause of blindness in many new-born babies. She found that it was caused by putting new-born babies in humidicribs on pure oxygen.

Sir Howard Florey (1898–1968), born in Adelaide, was the co-developer of penicillin. In 1945 he and Dr Ernst Chain were awarded the Nobel Prize for Medicine for their work. It is estimated that over 20 million lives have been saved as a result of the development of penicillin.

Dr William Griffith McBride was the Australian doctor who discovered the link between birth deformities and the drug thalidomide. Without his discovery there could have been millions more children born without normal arms and legs.

The Australia doctor, Sir Norman McAlister Gregg (1882–1966), was ridiculed by the world medical establishment when he discovered the link between rubella (German measles) and deformities in new-born babies. However, time has proved him right.

Before the voyages of Captain Cook it was generally accepted that sores, skin diseases and other illnesses were inevitable on long voyages. Cook proved that diseases were due to poor food, lack of exercise and filthy conditions. He was very particular about the cleanliness of his ships and personnel, and the men were fed malt tea and sauerkraut and later lime juice.

When the worldwide outbreak of bubonic plague reached Australia in 1900 the authorities had anticipated it. Many wharves were closed, slum areas cleaned and whitewashed, old and unsanitary houses demolished. A bounty of a penny each was put on rats.

HEALTH

Despite this, over 1000 cases were reported over the next decade. There was a later outbreak in 1921 but this was less serious.

Australia's worst poliomyelitis epidemic occurred in 1937. It was so bad that schools were closed in Victoria for several months.

According to the World Health Organisation, Australian men have a life expectancy of 69.3 years and women 76.4 years. This is the twelfth highest in the world for men, and the tenth highest for women.

The suicide rate in Australia is about 12 per 100,000 inhabitants per year. This puts us close to the world average and well under countries like Denmark and Switzerland with rates of over 20 per 100,000.

Here's a healthy statistic — Australia has the highest consumption of toothbrushes per person of any country in the world, and it is claimed that virtually all households buy toothpaste, as opposed to less than 90 per cent of households in most countries.

Heraldry

The present Australian coat of arms was granted by royal warrant in 1912. It replaced the original 1908 coat of arms which featured the kangaroo and emu half-facing outwards and the motto "Advance Australia". Although wattle flowers are sometimes shown around the coat of arms they are not really a part of it but simply decorations.

The Australian flag was not officially adopted by the Parliament until 1953. It was designed for Federation in 1901 as a composite of entries in a flag design competition. The only change since then was to change the Commonwealth star from five to seven points in 1909, to represent the State and territories.

Each Australian State has an officially proclaimed floral emblem.
Victoria • common heath (*Epacris impressa*)
New South Wales • waratah (*Telopea speciosissima*)
Queensland • Cooktown orchid (*Dendrobium biggibum*)
South Australia • Sturt's desert pea (*Clianthus formosus*)
Western Australia • kangaroo paw (*Anigozanthos manglesii*)
Tasmania • Tasmanian blue gum (*Eucalyptus globulus*)
Northern Territory • Sturt's desert rose (*Gossypium sturtianum*)
Australian Capital Territory • bluebell (*Wahlenbergia gloriosa*).

Five States have their own officially recognised fauna emblems.
Victoria • Leadbeater's possum (*Gymnobelideus leadbeateri*) and helmeted honeyeater (*Meliphaga cassidix*)
New South Wales • platypus (*Ornithorhynchus anatinus*) and kookaburra (*Dacelo gigas*)
Queensland • koala (*Phascolarctos cinereus*) and no bird emblem
South Australia • hairy-nosed wombat (*Lasiorhinus latifrons*) and the Australian magpie (*Gymnorhina tibicen*)
Western Australia • numbat (*Myrmecobius fasciatus*) and black swan (*Cygnus atratus*)
Tasmania • no fauna emblems
Northern Territory • red kangaroo (*Macropus rufus*) and wedge-tailed eagle (*Aquila audax*)
Australian Capital Territory • no fauna emblems.

Although there are no official emblems of Australia, the following are unofficially recognised: golden wattle (*Acacia pycnantha*); red kangaroo (*Macropus rufus*) and emu (*Dromaius novae-hollandiae*).

History

O.K.! WE DUMP THE STEAM LAUNCH! NOW WHAT ABOUT THE PIANO?!

There appears to be evidence that many people knew of Australia's existence well before Cook's voyage. As early as the second century, Ptolemy, the Greek mathematician, showed the western coast and described it as "Terra incognita".

The Chinese have a tradition that Australia was circumnavigated by Admiral Chang and an armada of over 60 ships in about 1470. Yamoda Nagamasa, a powerful Japanese pirate, landed frequently on the northern coast in the early 1600s. He called it "Sei-tso", the "South Land of Pearls".

Originally all land in Australia was Crown land belonging to the British Government. It was not until nearly 50 years after the first settlement, in 1831, that it became possible to privately own land in Australia.

In the early days of the settlement in New South Wales, the courts were made up of army officers, like military tribunals. It was not until 1839, some 51 years after the first settlement, that trial by jury was firmly established.

A map of the world published in 1536 in France shows Cape York and half of the Gulf of Carpentaria very accurately. The large island south of that region is described as "Jave La Grande". This is believed to be the oldest map showing Australia.

The first sighting of Australia by Europeans was probably by two Dutch sailors, Willem Jansz and Jan Lodewycksz. In March 1606 they sailed about 300 kilometres (186 miles) along the coast of Cape York Peninsula in the *Duyfken*, but did not realise that it was not part of the coast of New Guinea.

The first person, as far as we know, to penetrate the Antarctic Circle was Captain Cook in 1773, when he sailed around the Antarctic continent. The whalemen Bull and Borchgrevink were the first people to land on the Antarctic continent.

If the American War of Independence in 1776 had not ended transportation of 1000 convicts a year to America, the English Government might never have

HISTORY

established a penal settlement or a colony in Australia. The French would probably then have formed the first colonial settlements here and our whole history and culture might have been very different.

The establishment of the penal colony in New South Wales was illegal. It infringed the Charter of the East India Company who opposed its establishment vigorously. The East India Company was given rights over all land and trade from the East Indies to the coast of the Americas.

On 22 January 1788 Governor Arthur Phillip and his officers entered Port Jackson to find a suitable place of settlement for the First Fleet. As the boats passed Manly some Aborigines waded out and examined the boat. Phillip was so impressed with their confidence and manly behaviour that he named the place Manly Cove. Later that afternoon he was speared in the shoulder by an Aborigine in the same area.

Children at school in Portugal and Spain learn that Australian shores were first visited by Portuguese explorers in 1522. This was the year in which the adventurer Cristovas de Mendonca led an expedition to the Great South Land. It is believed that he mapped the east and south coasts of Australia as far as Kangaroo Island, but his exploits were kept secret because it was in territory granted by the Pope to Spain.

The second oldest settlement in Australia is Parramatta which lies 24 kilometres (15 miles) west of Sydney. It was settled in October 1788 about nine months after Sydney.

One of the noticeable things the early records describe about the transported convicts is their height. Most of them were very small, but this tended to be the case with people from the poorer classes at that time due to the poor standards of nutrition. Very few were above 5 feet 7 inches (1.70 metres).

The oldest town in Australia outside New South Wales is Hobart, Tasmania.

In the early days teams of convicts were used, particularly in Tasmania, to pull ploughs. Twenty or more convicts were chained together and a whip was used to "encourage" them.

When Port Arthur (Tas.) was a high security prison it was difficult to escape without crossing Eaglehawk Neck, the narrow isthmus connecting it to the main part of the island. Escape was prevented by a chain of savage, underfed dogs across the entire isthmus at 2 feet (60 centimetre) intervals.

The first settlement in Victoria was at Sorrento in October 1803. However, poor water supplies and hostile Aborigines forced the settlers to abandon the area in February 1804. The cemetery of the little settlement still remains at the spot.

It is a little difficult to see how Edward Henty could be Victoria's first permanent settler in 1834, when William Dutton was there to welcome him at the time. Dutton built a permanent home at Portland in 1833 but was probably the victim of a reluctance to recognise whaling stations as permanent residences and disapproval of his co-habitation with an Aboriginal woman.

When squatters' holdings were subdivided and sold by auction in the local town the squatters had "dummy" buyers bid on the land and then turn it over to them at a later date. Some "dummying" was done by relatives but

in many cases they were full-time professional "dummies".

Often white people were found living with the Aborigines around the Australian coast, years after surviving some forgotten shipwreck, although in many cases survivors were killed. The youngest survivor was William D'Oyley who was two years old in 1835 when he was purchased for a bunch of bananas from a tribe of Aborigines.

The first settler in the Canberra district was a Sydney merchant, Robert Campbell, who named his homestead "Duntroon" (now part of the military college). When the site for the capital had to be "within New South Wales and not less than 100 miles [160 kilometres] from Sydney", constant lobbying by the people of Queanbeyan led to Canberra being selected as the site.

When John Batman signed his treaty with the Aborigines he obtained 250,000 hectares (617,500 acres) of land covering the entire area of what is now Melbourne for some mirrors, knives and beads. However, he died only three years later.

Although Cook took possession of eastern Australia for Britain in 1770, it was another 59 years before Charles Fremantle took possession of the western region. This was despite the fact that European navigators knew of the western coasts as early as the first part of the 1600s.

Adelaide, capital of South Australia, was founded by Colonel Light in 1836. It was named after Queen Adelaide, consort of William IV who was at that time king of England.

A lot has been said about the transportation of the Tolpuddle Martyrs to Australia in 1834 for forming a trade union. However they all returned to England, after being pardoned in 1836. Back in England they were treated as heroes.

The first attempt to colonise northern Australia was made at Port Essington on the Cobourg Peninsula in 1838. A contingent of 300 people was landed and the township was named Victoria. By 1839 a severe hurricane, raging disease and personal feuds had all but destroyed the settlement. The Government tried to create a new Singapore but Asians would not live in the place. In 1846 the colony of North Australia was officially proclaimed, but shipping companies refused to make Port Essington a port of call. The colonists were withdrawn and re-settled in 1849.

That New South Wales once included Victoria and Queensland is known by most people with any knowledge of history. However, did you know that in 1840 and 1841 New Zealand was also a part of New South Wales?

When New South Wales and Victoria were separate colonies with different trade policies, smuggling was rife along the border. Victoria had stations to collect customs duties on goods brought in from New South Wales and there was a tremendous amount of smuggling across the Murray River.

The first explorer to use a camel was John Horrocks in 1840. Unfortunately, on one occasion when the poor beast knelt it lurched sideways, making a gun it was carrying discharge, and wounding Horrocks. He died about a month later and the poor camel was destroyed for its contribution to history.

In 1839 political prisoners were

HISTORY

transported from Canada to Australia. One group were French-Canadians who had taken part in Papineau's rebellion and were transported to Sydney. The others were sent after taking part in MacKenzie's rebellion in Northern Canada, and were taken to Tasmania.

The crew of H.M.S. *Beagle*'s sighting of natural bitumen near the Victoria River in the Northern Territory, in 1840, is the first record of any sign of oil in Australia.

When the last convicts were transported to Fremantle (W.A.) amongst them were 62 Fenians, or Irish republican rebels. In 1876 six of these Fenians were rescued by a ship sent by sympathisers in the United States. When the *Catalpa* returned to the United States with the Fenians they were greeted as heroes.

When the California gold rush was on in 1849 about 10 per cent of Sydney's population left for California. They must have been a bad lot because it is generally agreed that 12 of the first 16 men arrested in San Francisco's history were Australians.

The first gold found in Victoria was discovered at Warrandyte near Melbourne in July 1851. There is a memorial at the spot which is visited by thousands of people each year.

Over 40,000 Chinese came to the Victorian gold diggings in the period 1852 to 1858. Attempts were made to discourage Chinese immigration by charging a £10 per head landing tax. Further attempts to discourage the Chinese were made by landing them on remote beaches in South Australia. Undeterred, the Chinese simply walked overland to the gold fields, finding on the way the Canton Lead, which became the town of Ararat (Vic.).

Transportation of convicts to Western Australia continued well after it had ceased in all other colonies. This was at the request of the colonists themselves and due to the shortage of labour. The first convicts arrived in 1850, and the last in 1868.

South Australia was the only colony of Australia not to receive transported convicts to England. Altogether about 165,000 convicts were sent to Australia including 25,000 women. The average age of the convicts was 26 and in the whole period of transportation about 3000 died on the way out to Australia (which is about two per cent). Transportation ceased in 1868.

Although Mount Kosciusko is the highest mountain in Australia many historians believe that the mountain climbed by Polish explorer Strzelecki in 1840 and named for the great Polish patriot Thaddeus Kosciusko, was really Mount Townsend, the second highest mountain in Australia. Only later was it realised that the other peak was higher, and the name was transferred.

When the journal of Cook's voyage of 1770, kept by Sir Joseph Banks, was sold at Sotheby's in 1870, it fetched a wonderful £7.2.6. Nowadays it is in the Mitchell Library in Sydney and is regarded as priceless.

The first proposals for a Sydney Harbour Bridge were put forward in 1880, but work did not commence until 1926. The Sydney Harbour Bridge was opened in 1932.

At Federation, Western Australia was very reluctant to join the Commonwealth. In 1900 the Eastern Goldfields Separation Movement, centred in Kalgoorlie, moved to secede from Western Australia and join the

Federation if Western Australia did not join. Most of the people in the Separation Movement were from the eastern colonies and were dissatisfied with their treatment by the Western Australian Government. The Western Australian Government gave in to the pressure and joined the Federation.

From the time that the first settlement took place in Northern Australia until 1911, what is now the Northern Territory was part of South Australia. South Australian teachers, policemen and other government employees were used by the Northern Territory for many years after that.

South Australia was the first state to pass legislation relating to motor vehicles. In 1904 the speed limit was set at 12 miles per hour (20 kilometres per hour) in city streets and 4 miles per hour (6 kilometres per hour) in the main shopping areas between 7 p.m. and 10 p.m. Every car had to carry a disc showing the name and address of the owner, and the make of the car. Many people felt that these restrictions were a serious breach of civil rights, but there was still no requirement to drive on one particular side of the road.

Soon after Egon Kisch came to Australia in 1934, he led the protest marches against Hitler's rule of terror in Germany. He was regarded as a Communist and branded a liar by conservative politicians and the Press. The opinion of "responsible" people at that time was that Hitler had done a good job in Germany.

Australia was the fourth country after the U.S.S.R., U.S.A. and France to launch a satellite. It was launched from the Woomera rocket range (S.A.) in 1967, on a modified American Redstone rocket.

*Until 1918, when the name Australian Labor Party was adopted throughout Australia, the Labor Party (until 1906 spelt Labour) was variously named. For this reason Labor rather than ALP has been used here.
†The "fusion" of Free Traders and ex-Protectionist Tariff Reformers, and of Deakin's Protectionist followers.

HISTORY

PRIME MINISTERS OF AUSTRALIA

1 • Edmund Barton • Protectionist
   1 Jan. 1901 to 24 Sep. 1903
2 • Alfred Deakin • Protectionist
   24 Sep. 1903 to 27 Apr. 1904
3 • J. C. Watson • Labor*
   27 Apr. 1904 to 17 Aug. 1904
4 • G. H. Reid • Free Trade/Protectionist Coalition
   18 Aug. 1904 to 5 July 1905
5 • Alfred Deakin • Protectionist
   5 July 1905 to 13 Nov. 1908
6 • Andrew Fisher • Labor
   13 Nov. 1908 to 2 June 1909
7 • Alfred Deakin • Fusion†
   2 June 1909 to 28 Apr. 1910
8 • Andrew Fisher • Labor
   29 Apr. 1910 to 24 June 1913
9 • Joseph Cook • Liberal
   24 June 1913 to 17 Sep. 1914
10 • Andrew Fisher • Labor
   17 Sep. 1914 to 27 Oct. 1915
11 • W. M. Hughes • Labor
   27 Oct. 1915 to 14 Nov. 1916
12 • W. M. Hughes • National Labor
   14 Nov. 1916 to 17 Feb. 1917
13 • W. M. Hughes • Nationalist
   17 Feb. 1917 to 10 Jan. 1918
14 • W. M. Hughes • Nationalist
   10 Jan. 1918 to 9 Feb. 1923
15 • S. M. Bruce • Nationalist-Country Coalition *9 Feb. 1923 to 22 Oct. 1929*
16 • J. H. Scullin • Labor
   22 Oct. 1929 to 6 Jan. 1932
17 • J. A. Lyons • United Australia Party
   6 Jan. 1932 to 7 Nov. 1938
18 • J. A. Lyons • UAP-Country Coalition
   7 Nov. 1938 to 7 Apr. 1939
19 • Sir Earle Page • Country-UAP Coalition
   7 Apr. 1939 to 26 Apr. 1939
20 • R. G. Menzies • UAP
   26 Apr. 1939 to 14 Mar. 1940
21 • R. G. Menzies • UAP-Country Coalition
   14 Mar. 1940 to 28 Oct. 1940
22 • R. G. Menzies • UAP-Country Coalition
   28 Oct. 1940 to 29 Aug 1941
23 • A. W. Fadden • Country-UAP Coalition
   29 Aug. 1941 to 7 Oct. 1941
24 • J. Curtin • Labor
   7 Oct. 1941 to 21 Sep. 1943

25 • J. Curtin • Labor
   21 Sep. 1943 to 6 July 1945
26 • F. M. Forde • Labor
   6 July 1945 to 13 July 1945
27 • J. B. Chifley • Labor
   13 July 1945 to 1 Nov. 1946
28 • J. B. Chifley • Labor
   1 Nov. 1946 to 19 Dec. 1949
29 • R. G. Menzies • Liberal-Country Coalition
   19 Dec. 1949 to 11 May 1951
30 • R. G. Menzies • Liberal-Country Coalition
   11 May 1951 to 11 Jan 1956
31 • R. G. Menzies • Liberal-Country Coalition
   11 Jan. 1956 to 10 Dec. 1958
32 • R. G. Menzies • Liberal-Country Coalition
   10 Dec. 1958 to 18 Dec. 1963
33 • Sir Robert Menzies • Liberal-Country Coalition
   18 Dec. 1963 to 26 Jan. 1966
34 • H. E. Holt • Liberal-Country Coalition
   26 Jan. 1966 to 14 Dec. 1966
35 • H. E. Holt • Liberal-Country Coalition
   14 Dec. 1966 to 19 Dec. 1967
36 • J. McEwen • Liberal-Country Coalition
   19 Dec. 1967 to 10 Jan. 1968
37 • J. G. Gorton • Liberal-Country Coalition
   10 Jan. 1968 to 28 Feb. 1968
38 • J. G. Gorton • Liberal-Country Coalition
   28 Feb. 1968 to 12 Nov. 1969
39 • J. G. Gorton • Liberal-Country Coalition
   12 Nov. 1969 to 10 Mar. 1971
40 • W. McMahon • Liberal-Country Coalition
   10 Mar. 1971 to 5 Dec. 1972
41 • E. G. Whitlam • Labor
   5 Dec. 1972 to 19 Dec. 1972
42 • E. G. Whitlam • Labor
   19 Dec. 1972 to 11 Nov. 1975
43 • J. M. Fraser • Liberal-National Country
   11 Nov. 1975 to 22 Dec. 1975
44 • J. M. Fraser • Liberal-National Country Coalition *22 Dec. 1975 to 20 Dec. 1977*
45 • J. M. Fraser • Liberal-National Country Coalition *20 Dec. 1977 to 3 Nov. 1980*
46 • J. M. Fraser • Liberal-National Country Coalition *3 Nov. 1980 to 5 Mar. 1983*
47 • R. J. Hawke • Labor
   5 Mar. 1983 to 26 Oct. 1984
48 • R. J. Hawke • Labor
   26 Oct. 1984 to

Imports

"Clancy of the Overflow" was an Irishman, Thomas Gerald Clancy (1835–1914), who migrated to Melbourne in 1841. 'The Overflow" was a cattle station on the Lachlan River in New South Wales, and newspaper accounts of the epic cattle drive led by Clancy inspired "Banjo" Paterson's famous poem. They met in Sydney where Paterson became a witness to Clancy's will.

Johnny Famechon, world champion featherweight boxer from 1969 to 1970, was not born in Australia but in France in 1945. He came to Australia when he was four years old.

Harry M. Miller, theatrical producer, grazier, entrepreneur, promoter, was born in New Zealand.

Joh Bjelke-Petersen has been premier of Queensland since 1968. Few people realise that he was originally a New Zealander born at Dannevirke in the North Island.

Murray Rose who now lives permanently in the United States was a great swimmer for Australia, winning three gold medals at the 1956 Olympic Games and one in 1960. He broke 15 world records in his career, particularly at 800 metres and 1500 metres. However, he was born in Scotland and came to Australia as a baby.

Radio commentator and top-rating radio personality Derryn Hinch was born in New Zealand but took out Australian citizenship in 1981.

Mr Justice Higgins, famous for the Harvester industrial award of 1907 which established the basic wage, was born at Newtownwards in Ireland. He resigned in 1920 as a protest against political interference in the Arbitration Court.

It was not always easy for the vice-royals forced to live in the isolation of the colonies. In 1847 Governor Fitzroy of New South Wales lost his wife when she was killed in a carriage accident in the grounds of Government House, Sydney. He remarried on his return to

England, having complained of the lack of suitable colonial women.

Helen Morse, Australian actress, star of *A Town Like Alice* and so on, was born in England and came to Australia when she was three.

The great radio star Jack Davey came to Australia from Auckland (N.Z.) when he was 21 years of age. He had amazing ratings for his quiz and comedy shows on radio, and provided the commentary on film newsreels.

The archetypal Australian backblocks farmer was the character played by Bert Bailey in the Dad and Dave movies of the 1930s. But Bert Bailey was born in New Zealand and came to Australia as a child.

The famous Australian artist George Washington Lambert (1873-1930) was born in Leningrad, Russia, of American parents. He came to Australia with his mother, after his father's death in 1875.

Senator Colin Mason, one of the founders of the Australian Democrats, and before that of the Australia Party, was born in New Zealand.

"Breaker" Morant, the poet, horseman and victim of British politics was of course English, not Australian. He came to Australia at the age of 19, having spent five years in the Royal Navy. He came from a wealthy family and it has been claimed that he was sent out to the colonies because his family was angry about his gambling debts.

Heidelberg school artist Tom Roberts (1856-1931), famous for his impressionist landscapes, and in particular his painting "Bailed Up", was born in England.

Helena Rubinstein (1870-1965) sold her first cosmetics at Casterton in western Victoria, after arriving from Poland in her teens. She later opened a beauty salon in Collins Street, Melbourne and within two years expanded to larger premises. In 1908 she opened a salon in London, and moved to the United States in 1915 where she stayed. The company she started sells cosmetics in every developed country.

Adam Lindsay Gordon (1833-1870), famous in Australia as a poet, boxer and horseman, was not an Australian by birth. He was born in the Azores and settled in South Australia at the age of 20.

Industry

The first Australian-owned oil company was Neptune, which was a subsidiary of Lever and Kitchen, the soap company. It was started in 1909, but sold to the Shell Oil Company in 1926. All Australian oil was imported until 1964, when the Moonie oil field in Queensland commenced operations. With the Bass Strait field, and Barrow Island in Western Australia, Australia now produces about 80 per cent of its oil requirements.

Australia's largest company is the Broken Hill Proprietary Co. Ltd, (B.H.P.). It has virtual control of the iron and steel industry and controls an important share of the oil and gas production industry. However, it no longer operates any major activities at Broken Hill.

The Australian Ministry for Conservation produced figures which show that the packaging cost of some items exceeds the cost of the contents, particularly in the cosmetics area. Even with simpler products the packaging can account for a very high proportion of the cost. For instance, the packaging of beer in a tin plate can is 46 per cent of the cost, baby food in a glass jar 36 per cent, motor oil in a metal can 26 per cent, juice in a metal can 33 per cent, and frozen fish in a carton 5 per cent.

Sir Reginald Ansett who founded the Ansett transport empire started business as an impoverished bus operator with a daily bus service between Ballarat and Hamilton in western Victoria. He once offered a half share of his struggling business to a petrol station operator in return for credit for petrol purchases, but it was refused.

The commercial fruit with the largest production in Australia, both in tonnage and value, is the grape crop. It is used for wine, dried fruits, alcohol production and as a fresh fruit.

When the Canadian irrigation engineers, the Chaffey brothers, came at Prime Minister Deakin's invitation to establish an irrigation system at Mildura they were granted 100,000 hectares (247,100 acres) along the river. Although their company failed, the

INDUSTRY

scheme survived. One of their biggest achievements was to drive their steam traction engines overland from Adelaide to use in clearing the land.

Sir Frank Beaurepaire (1891–1956) represented Australia as a swimmer at the Olympic Games of 1908, 1920 and 1924. In 1934 he started the Olympic Tyre and Rubber Co. Ltd, which became one of Australia's largest companies.

Nearly 70 per cent of the tuna fish caught in Australia is caught by the SAFCOL fleet at Port Lincoln (S.A.). Many tourists visit Port Lincoln for the annual Tunarama festival each January, which marks the opening of the tuna season.

Axemen felling trees in hilly country often used the "drive" system. Trees on the slopes were partly cut through and left standing. Finally a tree at the top of the slope was felled making the lower trees topple onto each other in a spectacular chain reaction.

It used to be said that "Australia rides on the sheep's back", because wool was our main export. These days its value is only about half that of mineral ores, and less than that of coal, wheat and meat.

The major imports into Australia are petroleum products, motor vehicles, and electrical appliances in that order.

One feature of Australian rural industry is the high proportion of land which is still in its natural state. About 90 per cent of Australian farm land has not been developed and is still in its natural state. However, nearly all of the better pasture land has been improved.

Ampol Petroleum Ltd is the only Australian-owned oil company. It was founded by W. G. Walkley in 1936. All other major companies in the oil business are overseas-owned.

Australia's most important fishing industry is prawn production (about $100 million a year). Lobster (crayfish) production is second ($75 million) and tuna third. The fastest growing is South Australian blue grenadier fishing.

The Australian Agricultural Company was founded in 1823, largely as a result of a report by Commissioner Bigge. The original shareholders were the Attorney-General and Solicitor-General of England, 28 English parliamentarians, several directors of the Bank of England and the East India Company, Commissioner Bigge himself, the explorer John Oxley and eight members of the Macarthur family. It is still operating and now owns 20 properties. In 1974 it was listed on Australian Stock Exchanges, and control and management is now located in Australia.

In Australia 64 per cent of the land area is used for agriculture. Much of this is, however, marginal country with little production.

The Australian Mutual Provident Society (A.M.P.) is the oldest and largest life insurance company in Australia. It started business in 1849. By 1982 the total assets of the Society were $8620 million and its annual income was $1862 million. It is the biggest shareholder in Australian companies and has a significant interest in about 250 companies.

When the Australian Council of Trade Unions was formed in 1927 the Executive of the Australian Workers' Union, Australia's biggest union, feared

INDUSTRY

that it might be a device by which communists could take control of the union movement. So they refused to join and the A.W.U. did not become a member until January 1967.

Australia's energy sources at the moment are about 46 per cent from oil, 41 per cent from coal, eight per cent from natural gas, and five per cent from renewable sources like hydro-electricity and solar energy. At the present rate of use, oil and natural gas will run out in 70 years, but there is enough coal for the next 400 years or more.

In Canberra, the Australian capital, about 60 per cent of the city's workers are employed by the Government.

Bendigo (Vic.) no longer has any operative gold mines. If all of the 670 million grams (23 million ounces) of gold which were mined there were valued at today's prices, they would be worth about $12,000 million.

There was a great improvement in factory conditions after a severe bubonic plague outbreak in Australia's cities in 1900. Rubbish was removed, toilets improved and a rat destruction programme was carried out.

During the first World War supplies of aspirin from the German company, Bayer, were unavailable. No other company knew how to produce it and a reward was offered for the formula. It was eventually achieved by two chemists in Melbourne who had great difficulty in convincing anybody that they had done it. They eventualy formed Nicholas Pty Ltd, and their brand name "Aspro" is now world famous.

G. J. Coles & Co. Ltd was started by George Coles, born in Horsham (Vic.) in 1885. He and his brother opened a shop in Smith Street, Collingwood (Vic.) in 1913—a 3d., 6d., and 1/- store. By 1920 they also had shops in Prahran, Brunswick and the city. By 1928 they had 10 stores with an annual turnover of over £1 million. By 1936 they had 43 shops. Nowadays the company has over 1060 stores throughout Australia, including supermarkets, variety stores and specialty shops.

Coal was Australia's first export product. By 1800 it was being exported from Sydney to India and South Africa.

Dunlop Australia Ltd had a lot of firsts in Australian industry. It made the first Australian pneumatic tyres (1903), and the first Australian tennis balls (1908) and golf balls (1932). Brand names from companies in the Dunlop group include Dunlop, Slazenger, Ansell Rubber, Berlei, Hestia, Prestige and Holeproof.

Farmer and Co. Ltd was a leading Sydney department store until it merged with the Myer Emporium in 1961. It was established as a tiny drapery store in 1840 by Joseph and Caroline Farmer. By 1848, Joseph Farmer had retired, at 33 years of age, and brought his nephew William from England to run the business. Farmers was the first store in Sydney to put in large plate-glass front windows and held the first radio station licence with station 2FC which was sold to the A.B.C.

The first Sydney Stock Exchange was created informally by brokers meeting in Greville's Rooms near the present Martin Place. The Sydney Stock Exchange was formally set up in 1872. One of the early brokers was William Barton, father of Australia's first prime minister.

INDUSTRY 63

Woolworths Ltd is Australia's largest variety and grocery retailer. It operates in every State with over 1700 stores. Woolworths started business in 1924 and is not connected with the Woolworths company in Britain or the United States. Its founders simply copied the Woolworths name from the American company.

At one stage the koala fur industry was very important. In 1905, 60,000 koala pelts were sold in the Sydney fur market.

The 40-hour working week did not come into existence in Australia until 1948. The 44-hour week, which was normally five eight-hour days and a Saturday morning, was widely accepted in the 1920s but was not official until 1939. The 48-hour week of six eight-hour days (later five nine-hour days and Saturday morning) had become established from 1856 onwards. Before that people worked for 60 to 70 hours a week.

Thomas Elder, founder of Australia's largest pastoral firm, started in business by importing camels and breeding them at Umberatana in South Australia.

Australian workers have more paid holidays than workers in any other country. In Australia the average employee has 30 days per year, but in Sweden, for example, which is regarded as a workers' paradise, the average is 25 days.

Inventions

Sixteen-year-old farm boy Cliff Howard invented the first rotary hoe in 1919 by putting together bits and pieces taken from an old reaper and binder. His device was a metal plate to which L-shaped blades were attached. When this rotor was towed by a tractor, it turned and broke up the soil quickly and efficiently, and in such a way that side benefits were obtained: the dips created by the bite of blades into the subsoil prevented hard pan, and stopped loose soil from washing away in heavy rain. After World War I, Howard developed a commercially successful rotary hoe that had five sets of rotors and cultivated a 5 metre wide strip. Later improvements and refinements established the device as an essential piece of farm equipment.

People all round the world can now roll their furniture from room to room instead of lifting it, thanks to the castor invented by Australian George Shepherd. He first dreamed up the little device in the 1930s, and tested his prototypes by leaving them standing for six months bearing a load of one tonne. They showed no damage but the invention was slow to take on and Shepherd did not license its mass production until 1948. Since then the castors have been further improved so that they are now silent, dust-free, long-lasting, and move in any direction, without wobble. They are in universal use.

Wine in bottles turns sour within 48 hours of the bottle being opened. To overcome this problem Charles Malpas invented the plastic wine cask, a strong plastic bag tapped like a barrel which deflates as the wine is used. In this way, the wine is protected from contact with air and keeps for a very long time. Pak Pacific designed a strong cardboard box as a protective package for the plastic bag. Originally used by Wynn winemakers, the plastic bag enclosed in a protective cardboard box is now among the commonest methods of packaging wine for retail sale in Australia.

Mike Debenham's inventive contribution to modern life is the push-button can. It overcomes the problem of the litter-prone, as the buttons are hinged onto the can, unlike the throw-away ring pull. Opening Mike Debenham's can depends on two buttons. The pressure

FIRST TV REMOTE CONTROL

INVENTIONS

inside an aerated drink is quite high and a small button allows an easy first puncture. Then pushing down on the larger button to open the can is simple.

The pedal wireless, a radio using a pedal-powered generator, was invented by South Australian engineer Alfred Traeger, in 1926. It is still widely used in the outback.

Hugh Victor McKay (1865–1926) was the inventor of the combine harvester. His machine cut, threshed and cleaned the grain in one operation. His company became the Sunshine Harvester Co.

The totalisator was invented by an Australian, George Julius (1873–1946). He made his original model from old wheels and cogs, lead weights and piano wires. George Julius later became the first chairman of the C.S.I.R.O.

Walter Hume (1874–1943) designed the centrifugal method of making concrete pipes. His method is still employed all over the world. Hume had no formal education and started life as a plasterer.

An Australian, Anthony Mitchell, invented the thrust bearing in 1905. His invention was largely ignored until the first World War when a captured German U-boat was found to contain bearings of Mitchell's design.

The stump jump plough was invented in Australia in the 1870s by Richard Bowyer Smith (1838–1919). It allowed the plough to be used in fields where tree stumps had not been removed, which would have been impossible to cultivate before.

Dr Don Weiss of the C.S.I.R.O. developed the sirotherm process for purifying water using polymer resins. This is the most advanced method of water desalination in the world.

Mervyn Victor Richardson (1896–1972) who founded Victa Ltd, invented the modern form of motor mower. For many years he manufactured the mowers in his backyard at Concord in Sydney, before forming a public company in 1953 which has since maintained market leadership in the industry. He was nearly 60 years old when he formed the company. Before that he sold them for about $20 each to friends and neighbours.

The Repco spinner invented in Australia by David Henshaw in 1970 automatically creates two-ply yarn by a twisting process, cutting down the production costs.

The Interscan method for flight-plan control of aeroplanes during landing and taking off is now being installed all over the world. It was invented by Dr Paul Wild of the C.S.I.R.O.

When people are poisoned or food is contaminated a machine is needed that locates and measures small traces of metals such as lead, thallium or cadmium. Sir Alan Walsh, an Australian, invented the atomic absorption spectrophotometer which does this work and is used all over the world.

Australian astronomers were the first to detect quasars (quasistellar radio sources) and have also discovered more than half of the pulsars so far detected. This is probably due to the clarity of the skies and our domination of the science in the southern hemisphere.

Lifestyle

Only recently has the old practice of "tin-kettling" newly married couples disappeared. Even in the 1960s it was common for friends to visit the newlyweds' house late at night banging kettles, tins and other metal objects as a way of bringing them good luck.

The old swagmen could not afford luxuries like socks. They used "toe rags", pieces of old rag wrapped around the feet. Particularly favoured for their comfort were old flour bags.

The famous Australian slouch hat originated with Colonel Tom Price of the Victorian Mounted Rifles which he formed as a private force in 1885. The brim was turned up on the right-hand side so that soldiers could shoulder arms without knocking their hats off.

Melbourne is the only major city in the world which has a holiday for a horse-race. When the Melbourne Cup is run on the first Tuesday in November most people have a holiday. In earlier times it was described as Sunday School Picnic Day so as not to offend the sensibilities of the more "concerned" members of the community.

The most unusual thing about housing in Australia is the high level of home ownership. About 72 per cent of home occupiers own or are buying their homes, but in recent years the proportion has slowly declined.

The Australian Post Office handles about 11 million pieces of mail every weekday.

Separate Australian citizenship never existed until the Australian Citizenship Act of 1948. Until then all Australians were simply "British subjects".

Despite a population density of less than two people per square kilometre (.386 square mile) Australia is one of the world's most urbanised countries. Less than 15 per cent of the population live in rural areas.

LIFESTYLE

About 20 per cent of Australians go on to tertiary education. This is lower than in most comparable countries and well under the 55 per cent in the U.S.A.

It is estimated that nearly half the Australian population never read a book. On average Australians read about three books a year which is slightly above the world average.

Of all the developed countries Australia has the lowest percentage of people who travel abroad each year (only 15 per cent of the population). This compares with 74 per cent in Switzerland and 30 per cent in the U.S.A. It is probably due to our remote location.

Duelling was used to settle disputes between gentlemen until the 1850s but there was seldom any injury suffered as the weapons were inaccurate, and the intention was only to wound, not kill. In Melbourne in 1840 two squatters—Peter Snodgrass and William Ryrie—fought a duel. Before the signal was given to fire, Snodgrass's pistol discharged, shooting off the end of his big toe. Ryrie fired into the air as the unfortunate Snodgrass sat clutching his foot. Honour was satisfied.

The building of large expensive garages just to house motor cars probably goes back to the days when the motor car replaced the horse. Horses had to be kept under cover at night and given comfortable stabling. Garages in houses built in the 1920s are usually separate structures built well away from the house. This was because the shortage of petrol stations led to people storing petrol in their garages, and councils had regulations preventing garages from being constructed adjacent to houses because of the fire danger.

Up until the time television started in 1956, euchre nights were very popular. People would play cards until about 10 p.m., followed by some dancing to radio or records. It all seems so quaint now, but at the time it seemed wonderful.

One-hour daylight saving was introduced in Melbourne to assist in a fuel crisis in January 1942. It was also used in 1943 and the first part of 1944, and then it ceased. It has recently been restored in Victoria and introduced in all states except Queensland and Western Australia.

Apex Club is an Australian organisation which was started in 1931 by three Geelong (Vic.) architects, Ewan Laird, John Buchan and Langham Proud. The Apex Club is devoted to developing fellowship and service to the community. It is non-political and has no particular religious affiliation. It is restricted to men aged 18 to 35 who work in business, a trade, or profession, and members must retire at 40.

The grooms who worked for Cobb & Co. in the 1850s attended the horses, inspected and replaced the harness and cleaned the coaches at all hours of the day and night for £8 ($16) a month. In most cases they slept in the stables. Food was provided, though.

In 1938 Victoria held a referendum on the prohibition of alcohol. It was lost by a substantial majority but some local councils in Melbourne still established policies preventing the licensing of hotels. Even today the area around Box Hill and Balwyn has no hotels.

The capital cities of Australia were not fully linked with an airmail service until 1938.

The old-age pension was introduced in 1909. It was set at about a quarter of the average working man's wage. It was intended as a charity for those who were unable to support themselves in any other way and was not intended as a right at all. In the early days many people who had a right to it would not take it, out of pride.

In June 1981, at the Census, Australia's population was 14,574,488. Present estimates are that it will not reach 20 million until about 2025.

As far as the Australian Bureau of Statistics can ascertain about 25 per cent of Australia's households have a firearm in their possession.

In recent years in Australia there have been roughly half as many deaths each year as births. Despite this, population growth has been very slow.

Every year over 2 million people arrive in Australia (including residents returning from holiday). About the same number leave each year but there is a slight net gain due to migration.

Since the second World War about 3.7 million migrants have settled in Australia. About 20 per cent of Australia's population were born overseas and another 20 per cent have at least one parent born overseas.

Australian citizenship may be obtained by birth in Australia, by birth to an Australian parent at any place in the world or by naturalisation. It is not automatically obtained by marrying an Australian citizen, but it is automatically obtained by being born here even if neither parent is a citizen.

Queenslanders originated the idea of keeping houses cool by building them on high stumps to enable the air to circulate completely around the house.

98.8 per cent of Australians who stated their religion in the 1981 census claimed to be Christians. The largest group was the Anglicans (36 per cent) followed by Roman Catholics (33 per cent). Over a million Australians stated that they had no religion. This figure has grown faster than the figures for any religious group.

The Australian centre of the Baha'i faith is at Ingleside near Sydney. The faith originated in Persia in 1844 and was founded in Australia in 1920. Its adherents are mainly Australian-born and are attracted by its communal attitude and simple lifestyle.

Australia is still the only country in the world where all children from seven to 14 years of age are enrolled in full-time education.

BIG THINGS IN A BIG COUNTRY

Imaginana is a word invented to describe strange blown-up products of the Australian imagination. Examples of Imaginana are the Big Banana (Coffs Harbour), the Big Pineapple (Nambour), the Big Humpty Dumpty Who Talks (Mildura), the Big Black Marlin (Cairns), the Big Penguin (Penguin, Tasmania).

Australia's sweeping landscape is rich in big things, which is surely a reflection of pride in the Aussie habitat. We do, after all, live on the biggest island on Earth. The country is chokkers with other big attractions. There are the natural ones like Ayers Rock and the Great Barrier Reef. And then there are the man-made variety. The Land Down Under is bristling with giant cows, bulls and sheep, big

LIFESTYLE

lobsters, big chooks and buffalos, big stubbies and big strawberries.

Identified categories include fact and fiction (boots to bunyips); sport (big football, bowling pins and jumbo tennis racquets); people such as Captain Cook and the big gold panner; animals; aquatic life, ranging from cod to crustaceans; and fruit and vegetables.

Many of the Imaginana pieces are not easily recognisable as Australiana. The theory is that overseas visitors can readily relate to a Big Apple, but could they comprehend the niceties of a Big Pavlova? Rather than risk misunderstanding and even mirth, Imaginana artists and patrons have tended to stick to big things considered to be internationally acceptable.

To counteract this cultural drift, an encouraging link with our goldmining past was forged at the Gold Panner Motor Inn, near Bathurst in N.S.W., when the proprietor risked overseas criticism by commissioning a Big Gold Panner to advertise his motel, instead of the more usual neon sign.

Other evidence of renewed national pride is emerging and in the ranks of Australia's "biggies" listed below we may soon see the Giant Gumnut, the Big Thong and the Great Grey *Antechinus*.

A List of Big Things

Fact and Fiction

The Big Boot • Chermside, Brisbane • *5 m x 3 m x 1.5 m*
The Big Copper Stubby Cooler • Smithville, Qld • *2 m diameter*
The Big Deck Chair • Mildura, Vic. • *4.6 m long, 4 m high, 2.4 m wide*
The Big Eltham Barrel • Eltham, Vic. • *27 m diameter, capacity: 800 million litres*
The Big Ettamogah Bunyip • Albury, N.S.W. • *2 m high*
The Big Hand on the Walking Stick • Collingwood, Melbourne • *2 storeys high*
The Big Hanwood Barrel • Griffith, N.S.W. • *capacity: 60-70 people*
The Big Humes Pipe • North Nambour, Qld • *outside diameter: 1.7 m, 2.4 m long*
The Big Jam Tin • South Yarra, Melbourne • *3 m diameter, 4.5 m high*
The Big Lifesaver • whereabouts unknown • *3.5 m diameter*
The Big Long Bar • Mildura, Vic. • *90.7 m long*
The Big Mower • Beerwah, Qld • *3 x 3.6 m base, 11.5 m high*
The Big Murray Bridge Bunyip • Murray Bridge, S.A. • *very big*
The Big Shoe • Port Macquarie, N.S.W. • *6 m long, 5 m high, 2 m wide*
The Big Softdrink Bottle • Freshwater Creek, Vic. • *17,500 bottles*
The Big Windmill • Diamond Creek, near Melbourne • *15 m high, 17 m blade span*
The Big Wine Bottle • Griffith, N.S.W. • *4 m diameter, 17 m long, 35 tonnes weight*
The World's Biggest Talking Humpty Dumpty • Mildura, Vic. • *5 m high, 3 m wide, 1 tonne weight*

Animals

The Big Braford Bull • Rockhampton, Qld • *25% larger than life*
The Big Brahmin Bull • Rockhampton, Qld • *25% larger than life*
The Big Brontosaurus • Coonabarabran, N.S.W. • *23 m long*
The Big Chook • Blackwood, Vic. • *2 m high*
The Big Cow • North Nambour, Qld • *10.8 m long, 7.9 m high*
The Big Dinosaur • Nambour, Qld • *11 m high*

LIFESTYLE

The Big Horse • Vineyard, N.S.W. • *11 m high*
The Big Merino Ram • Goulburn, N.S.W. • *12 m high, 17 m long*
The Big Penguin • Penguin, Tas. • *3 m high*
The Big Santa Gertrudis Bull Rockhampton, Qld • *25% larger than life*
The Big Sheep • Campbell Town, Tas. • *4 m high*
The World's Biggest Water Buffalo • Winnellie, N.T. • *4 m long, 8 m high, 14 tonnes weight*

Sport
The Big Bowling Ball • Lake Cathie, N.S.W. • *2 m diameter, 3 m high*
The Big Bowling Pin • Alexandra Headland, Qld • *4.5 m high*
The Big Football • Wagga Wagga, N.S.W. • *2.5 m long*
The Big Golf Ball • Spring Valley, Melbourne • *4 m diameter, 9 tonnes weight*

Aquatic Life
The Big Black Marlin • Cairns, Qld • *20 m high*
The Big Lobster • Kingston, S.A. • *17 m high, 14 m leg span, 4 tonnes weight*
The Big Murray Cod • Wagga Wagga, N.S.W. • *9 m high, 3 m long*
The Big Rainbow Trout • Horsham, Vic. • *8 m long, 1.8 m high*
The Big Shell • Tewantin, Qld • *7.3 m high*
The Big Tocumwal Cod • Tocumwal, N.S.W. • *6.5 m long, 2.3 m high*
The World's Biggest Trout • Adaminaby, N.S.W. • *12 m high*

Fruit and Vegetables
The Big Apple • Batlow, N.S.W. • *3.6 m high*
The Big Banana • Coffs Harbour, N.S.W. • *13 m high, 11 tonnes weight*
The Big Cane • Childers, Qld • *9 m high*
The Big Nambour Pineapple • Nambour, Qld • *5.5 m high*

The Big Potato • Robertson, N.S.W. • *12.2 m long, 3.7 m high, 3.7 m wide*
The Big Fruit Bowl • Kurrajong, N.S.W. • *2.5 m high*
The Big Potplant • Nerang, Qld • *5 m high*
The Big Strawberry • South of Brisbane • *6 m high, 7.5 m wide*
The World's Biggest Orange • Riverland, S.A. • *12 m diameter, 18 m high*
The World's Biggest Pineapple • Gympie, Qld • *7.6 m diameter, 16 m high, 257 tonnes weight*

People
The Big Captain Cook • Cairns, Qld • *14 m high*
The Big Chef's Head • Scoresby, Vic. • *2.5 m high*
The Big Digger • The Entrance, N.S.W. • *3.6 m high*
The Big Gold Panner • Bathurst, N.S.W. • *4.5 m high*
The Big King Neptune • Yanchep Sun City Resort, W.A. • *10 m high*
The Big Pirate • Scoresby, Vic. • *4 m high*
The Big Scottish Piper • Medindie, S.A. • *4 m high*

THE AUSTRALIAN YOUTH HOSTELS ASSOCIATION

The first Youth Hostels in Australia were established in the early 1940s in Victoria, New South Wales and Tasmania. In 1947, the Australian Youth Hostels Association was formed to co-ordinate the efforts of the various State Associations and to represent Australia internationally. In that year, A.Y.H.A. was admitted as a member of the International Youth Hostel Federation (I.Y.H.F.) This affiliation allows members of the A.Y.H.A. to use Youth Hostels overseas, as guests of that association, and similarly, hostellers from overseas can use Australian hostels.

The following is a list of Australian hostels.

New South Wales Hostels
Armidale
Bega
Broken Hill
Bundanoon
Byron Bay
Canberra
Carrington
Coffs Harbour
Coonabarabran
Deniliquin
Garie Beach (Royal National Park)
Gerringong
Girvan
Katoomba
Lightning Ridge
Murwillumbah
Narooma
Narrandera
Nimbin
North Springwood
Nowra
Orange
Scone
Pittwater
Sydney (Forest Lodge, Dulwich Hill, Glebe Pt.)
Tenterfield
Thredbo
Wagga Wagga
Wauchope

Northern Territory Hostels
Alice Springs
Darwin
Glen Helen
Hamilton Downs
Katherine
Mataranka
Pine Creek
Tennant Creek
Timber Creek
Kakadu National Park

Queensland Hostels
Airlie Beach
Brisbane
Cairns
Cape Tribulation
Gold Coast (Southport)
Gold Coast (Surfers Paradise)
Gold Coast (Coolangatta)
Great Keppel Island
Hervey Bay
Jondaryan
Kuranda
Longreach
Mackay
Mackay City
Magnetic Island
Maroochydore
Mission Beach (Bingil Bay)
Mount Isa
Noosa
Noosa (Sunshine Beach)
Rockhampton
Roma
Sapphire
Warwick
Woody Point

South Australian Hostels
Adelaide
Beachport
Inman Valley
Kersbrook
Loxton
Mylor
Port Vincent
Wirrabara

Tasmanian Hostels
Bicheno
Bruny Island
Coles Bay
Cygnet
Deloraine
Devonport
Hobart (Bellerive)
Hobart (New Town)
Launceston City
Lune River
Mount Field National Park
New Norfolk
Oatlands
Port Arthur
Scamander
Sheffield
St. Marys
Strahan
Swansea
Triabunna
Wynyard

Victorian Hostels
Bairnsdale
Ballarat
Beechworth
Camperdown
Echuca
Emerald
Geelong
Halls Gap
Mallacoota
Melbourne
Mt. Baw Baw
Mt. Buller
Portarlington
Philip Island (Cowes)
Portable Hostels
Port Fairy
Warburton
Warrandyte

Western Australian Hostels
Albany
Augusta
Bridgetown
Coolgardie
Denmark
Dingo Flat (Tingledale)
Esperance
Fremantle
Geraldton
Mundaring Weir
Noggerup
Northam
Pemberton
Perth City
Piesse Brook
Quindalup
Toodyay
York

Media

A study made by Professor Henry Mayer revealed that on the average in newspapers the advertisements take up 58.6 per cent of space, which leaves 41.4 per cent for the news! Of this 7.4 per cent is used for foreign news, 7.4 per cent for political-social-economic news, 10.8 per cent for other news—and 15 per cent for sport.

There are over 1000 magazines and periodicals regularly produced in Australia. Nearly a quarter of them are produced by trade unions, political parties and trade and commercial organisations. The biggest-selling magazine is the *New Idea* which has sold over a million copies of one issue. The *Australian Women's Weekly* which is now a monthly magazine was the leader for many years.

Television began in Australia in 1956, and the first big media event was the Olympic Games in Melbourne. People stood in crowds on the footpaths watching television sets in shop windows.

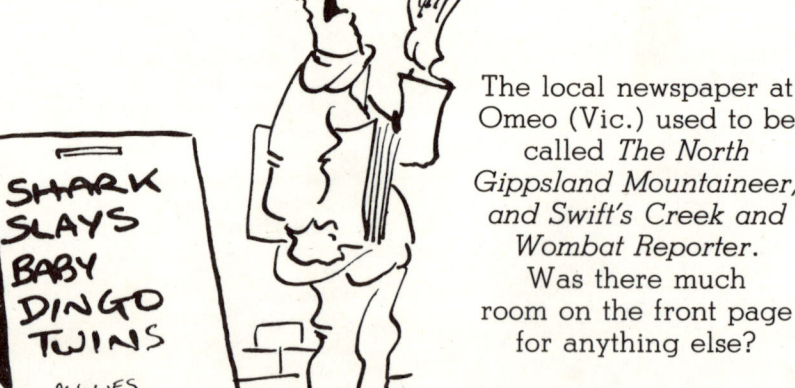

The local newspaper at Omeo (Vic.) used to be called *The North Gippsland Mountaineer, and Swift's Creek and Wombat Reporter*. Was there much room on the front page for anything else?

The first regular user of "talk-back" sessions on radio was Mike Walsh who was a top-rating radio personality before going into television.

The Melbourne *Sun News-Pictorial* has the biggest circulation of any newspaper in Australia. Its average daily sales over many years have been around 670,000 copies.

When radio first started in Australia in 1923, it was on the "closed set system". You had to buy a receiver which could tune in to only one station. However, this system was not a financial success as only 1200 people bought them. In 1924 the "open set" receivers, which could pick up all stations, went on sale.

Sydney's radio station 2UW has broadcast without a break since 22 February 1935—twenty-four hours a day for about 50 years.

In 1896 John Norton the editor of the Sydney *Truth* was charged with sedition (but was acquitted) when he wrote: "God Save the Queen, so as to keep her rascal of a turf-swindling, card-sharping, wife-debauching, boozing rowdy of a son, Albert Edward, Prince of Wales, off the throne." She could not be saved forever and Edward VII ruled from 1901 to 1911.

The Age, which is now arguably the best newspaper in the country, nearly folded after two months. Its owners, the Cook brothers, campaigned for the diggers' rights and *The Age* was regarded as so radical that it could not attract advertising revenue. However, after announcing that it would close in December 1854, it was saved by the Syme brothers, who built it into an influential newspaper.

The radio serial *Blue Hills* (first known as *The Lawsons*) written by Gwen Meredith ran continually on ABC Radio for 33 years, ending in 1976.

There are over a million licensed CB radio transceivers in Australia. Between 1958 and 1977 they were illegal but were legalised, with limitations, in 1977.

When the Overland Telegraph Line from Port Augusta (S.A.) to Darwin (N.T.) was opened in 1872 it gave direct access to news events in Europe. However, only one news service could use it at a time. So the service which first logged the story would do anything to prevent its competitors from using the line. One tactic was to relay the story to Australia then tell the telegraph operator to relay a couple of books of the Bible to give them a headstart over the opposition.

The A.B.C. got into the radio business by buying what were known as the A-class stations in 1929. A-class stations were allowed only 15 minutes of advertising each evening and received part of the licence fees paid by listeners. The so-called B-class stations had unlimited advertising.

In the early days of the first colony the only newspaper, the *Sydney Gazette* published by the Government Printer was censored to avoid any anti-administration material appearing. This censorship existed until 1824, and Governor Darling fought bitterly to restore censorship between 1826 and 1830, but failed.

The first demonstration of television in Australia was at the studios of Melbourne radio station 3UZ, on 10 January 1929.

Money

In the 1850s some of the gold miners around Beechworth (Vic.) who had struck it rich had money to burn. It was quite usual for them to light their pipes with £5 notes. Others made a show of their wealth by putting solid gold horseshoes on their horses.

Australia did not produce its own coins until 1910. Before that English coinage was used although some of it was produced at mints in Australia. Federal bank notes were not printed until 1913; before that each bank produced its own notes.

The first Australian dollar was the holey dollar. In 1814 coinage was in short supply and the Spanish silver dollar was worth five shillings. The Government removed a circular piece from the centre which was called the dump. The dump was issued as a quarter dollar, at one shilling and threepence, and the dollar with the hole was re-issued for five shillings. They remained in circulation into the 1830s.

Before Federation the major sources of income for the Australian colonies were railway revenues (which represented over 50 per cent), customs and excise duties and sale of Crown land to settlers. There were no income taxes because it was believed that people would rebel against such impositions.

Apart from the stock exchanges in the capital cities there are still five country stock exchanges in Australia. They are located at Ballarat and Bendigo (Vic.), Newcastle (N.S.W.), Rockhampton (Qld) and Launceston (Tas.).

The wealth of a country is measured by taking its total income and dividing it by the population. On this basis Australia ranks about 14th behind the United Arab Emirates, Qatar, Kuwait, Lichtenstein, Switzerland, Sweden, Monaco, U.S.A., Canada, West Germany, Luxembourg, Belgium and New Caledonia.

A pearl found at Broome in 1918 was the size of a sparrow's egg and weighed over 100 grains. Its value was estimated at nearly $30,000.

The Bank of New South Wales, which became the Westpac Banking Corporation in 1982, is Australia's oldest bank. It was formed in Sydney in 1817 which also makes it Australia's oldest company.

Mysteries

HAUNTED HOSE
WODONGA 1924

The ship *Selena* was carrying cedar and pine logs from Brisbane to Sydney, but disappeared without trace in 1847. The weather was fine and searchers found no sign of the vessel. Eighteen months later she was found at Keppel Bay, 350 kilometres (217 miles) north (in the wrong direction). She was undamaged and her boats were still in the davits. The log, papers and the crew's personal possessions were all intact. No trace was ever found of the crew or their passenger. Nobody has any idea what happened to them.

In 1846 workmen excavating for a lime kiln at Limeburner's Point, Geelong, uncovered some ancient iron keys in a shaft they had dug about 4.6 metres (15 feet) into the ground. How long must they have been there to be buried by so much earth—and how did they get there?

At Bittangabee Bay (N.S.W.) there are the ruins of what appears to have been an old fort. The buildings have been made from local stone and rubble with seashell mortar. It is believed to be the remains of a 16th-century Portuguese fort built hundreds of years before Cook "discovered" eastern Australia.

In the Tiger Hotel at Tantanoola (S.A.) is the stuffed hide of the Tantanoola tiger. It is unclear whether this creature which was shot in 1895 was a dingo or a deformed dog, but it was responsible for massive sheep killings and was credited with supernatural powers. It was definitely not a thylacine (Tasmanian tiger). Recently "experts" have declared that it was a Syrian wolf. How or why a Syrian wolf came to be wandering the wilds of South Australia in 1895 is unexplained.

Australia has its own equivalent of the "yeti" and American "sasquatch" or "big foot". The "yowie" has been sighted frequently in the mountainous forests of the Great Dividing Range. It is said to be about two metres high, covered in brown hair with a head like a cave man.

Dr George Bass, who with Matthew Flinders discovered Bass Strait,

disappeared while aboard the brig *Venus* which left Sydney in 1803. The ship disappeared without trace and was probably wrecked on the south coast of New Zealand. It has been claimed, however, that he was captured by pirates and sent to work in the Chilean mercury mines.

An old story claims that there is a ghost that walks the grounds of Yarralumla House, the governor-general's Canberra residence. It is reputedly the ghost of an Aboriginal murdered by a gang of bushrangers for swallowing a diamond that they wanted. He is supposed to have been buried under a large deodar tree in the gardens which has long since gone. Occasionally diamond hunters tried to dig for the treasure.

South of Yallourn in Victoria is a small range of hills called the Haunted Hills. In the old days it was claimed that cattle would not feed there and there is evidence that cattle often stampeded in the area without apparent reason. Strange echoing noises like hoofbeats were often heard. A theory has been suggested that in some places the brown coal which underlies the area may have been burnt out, leaving hollow areas which echo sounds from some distance away.

Melbourne's Princess Theatre is said to be haunted by the ghost of the Italian bass, Federici. Federici was playing Mephistopheles in Gounod's *Faust* in which he was required to disappear through a trapdoor. Unfortunately he died from a fall during his disappearance act and his ghost is said to haunt the theatre.

In the Campbelltown district of New South Wales in June 1826 a convict called Worral murdered a man called Fisher and threw his body into a swamp next to a creek. Later a farmer, John Farley, claimed to have seen the ghost of Fisher, and an investigation found the body. Worral was arrested but swore that Fisher had returned to England under a false name. He was found guilty and admitted his crime before execution. Since then many people have reported appearances of the ghost.

In 1941 two fishermen fishing off the Queensland coast saw what appeared to be a sea serpent. "The Mooloolabah Monster" was estimated to be 18 metres (60 feet) in length, with red and grey markings, and a huge red beard. Other fishermen claimed to have seen it off Townsville in 1934.

It is "Goobang Mick" Connolly who is supposed to have betrayed the bushranger Ben Hall to the police in 1865. His wife Mary Connolly was in love with Ben Hall and was carrying his child when she saw his body riddled with 32 bullet wounds. When her son was born he had 32 birthmarks, corresponding with the bullet wounds on Hall's body. Later he toured Australia as a sideshow freak, billed as "The Leopard Boy".

When Judge Barry passed the death sentence on Ned Kelly in 1880, the infamous bushranger said to him "I will see you where I am going!" Judge Barry died only 25 days later, two days after Ned Kelly was hanged.

Australites are small glass-like stones found mainly in south-western Australia. They have been called "button stones", "emu stones" and "blackfellows' buttons". Some scientists believe that they are tiny meteorites, others believe that they are formed by the impact of meteorites on the earth and yet others that they have nothing to

do with meteorites but were formed by volcanic action.

In these days of sensationalist reports of U.F.O.s we sometimes laugh off reports of strange lights following people for long distances on straight roads. However, the Aborigines have been aware of such lights for centuries. They called them the min min.

It is still not understood why the Blue Lake at Mount Gambier (S.A.) changes colour from grey to blue in November each year, then back to grey in March. In its blue phase it is a magnificent bright blue regardless of the weather.

Aborigines used the magic ritual of pointing the bone at their enemies to cause their death. The man who carried out the ritual pointed a stick or preferably a bone at his enemy while chanting a traditional song. He was always very careful because of the belief that if he made a mistake the curse would fall on himself instead of his enemy.

When the *Loch Ard* was wrecked near Port Campbell (Vic.) in 1878 a magnificent Minton porcelain figure of a peacock was washed up on the beach in its crate, completely undamaged. It is now on exhibition in the Maritime Village at Warrnambool (Vic.). Nobody knows how it managed to survive such violent events.

Joseph Samuels was due to be hung for stealing at Sydney in 1803. The noose was placed around his neck and the cart driven from under him, but the rope snapped. A new rope was used to make a new noose and the cart was driven off again, but the rope loosened and he was left with his feet dangling on the ground. By this time Samuels was unconscious, but a third rope was obtained and his body was supported by policemen and then allowed to drop. The rope snapped again. Samuels was given a reprieve as "the man they couldn't hang", but later turned to crime again and was lost at sea in a stolen boat.

Less than a week after the First Fleet landed at Botany Bay a large piece of fishing net was found on the beach. It was not of European design and was made of twine in a small mesh unlike the Aboriginal nets. Nobody knows where it came from.

In the Darling River area of New South Wales there are strange cylindrical and conical stones covered in markings and decorations. These cylcons, as they are called, are thought to have been related to the ceremonial rites of the local Aboriginal tribes.

Recently a group of Americans have begun searching for a gold-covered pyramid which they believe is located in Queensland. So if you are going there on holiday, take a shovel.

Names

If King O'Malley (1853–1953) the Canadian-born Australian politician, later minister for Home Affairs, had been given his way the Australian capital would have been called "Shakespeare" and would have been located at Dalgety (N.S.W.).

We are all familiar with the Australian features named after Queen Victoria including Victoria, Queensland and Queenstown (Tas.), but how many people realise that Lake Alexandrina at the mouth of the Murray River (S.A.) is another. She was christened Alexandrina Victoria.

New South Wales obtained its name because Captain Cook thought that the land looked a great deal like South Wales, when he made his only visit in 1770.

Most people have heard of the "Rats of Tobruk" but Japanese radio referred to the Australian defenders of Papua and New Guinea, based at Port Moresby in 1942, as the "Mice of Moresby".

The name Dutigallar, Dutigalla, or in its present spelling Doutta Galla is often seen around Melbourne. It was the name of the Aboriginal tribe who lived in the Port Phillip area and "sold" the land to John Batman.

Evan Nepean (1752–1822) after whom the river near Sydney is named, was the senior British public servant in charge of the First Fleet's voyage. When a site was being selected for the penal colony he favoured East Africa, but it was ruled out because of the fear of disease. He later became governor of Bombay.

Some Australian places have obtained their names in strange ways. When the Excelsior Land, Investment and Building Company subdivided land on the shore of Lake Macquarie, near Newcastle (N.S.W.) in 1887 there was a world champion rower, Edward Hanlon, visiting Sydney at the time. He was born in Toronto (Canada). So what was more obvious than to call the town Toronto.

Melbourne was first called Bearbrass, but at one stage it was proposed (in 1835) that it be called Batmania after its

NAMES

alleged founder, John Batman. The name "Melbourne" was given to the city by Governor Bourke in 1837 after Lord Melbourne who was then the British prime minister. Melbourne is the name of an English village and is old English for "mill stream".

The official name of the Flinders Naval Depot in Victoria is H.M.A.S. *Cerberus*. The name is taken from the H.M.V.S *Cerberus*, pride of the Victorian navy. It was a monitor mounted with four massive 18 inch (46 centimetre) guns. It was later renamed H.M.A.S. *Platypus II* when taken over by the Commonwealth Navy. It was eventually scrapped and sunk to become part of a breakwater at Black Rock (Vic.) where it still lies. Suggestions that it be raised and restored do not seem to have made much progress.

Originally Ballarat was called "Yuille's Swamp". The word "Ballarat" is probably derived from an Aboriginal word meaning "resting place".

The name of Australia was nearly set as "Federal Dominion of Australia" because it was felt that "Commonwealth" sounded too republican in its connotations, since it was the word used by Cromwell after the English Civil War. However, it was accepted by the delegates that it meant a State in which everybody had a say in what was done, and adopted at a convention in 1891.

The Victorian town of Bairnsdale was named after a homestead of that name in the area. The Aboriginal name was Wy-yung meaning "wild duck". The homestead was so named by its Scottish owner because "bairns (babies) arrived annually with unfailing regularity".

Probably the shortest place name in Australia is A.1. This tiny settlement near Woods Point (Vic.) takes its name from the gold mining company which still operates nearby.

The longest place name in Australia is the salt lake, Lake Cadibarrawirracanna near Lake Eyre in South Australia.

The northernmost part of the Northern Territory, Arnhem Land, is named after the Dutch vessel, *Arnhem*, which discovered the area in 1642 when blown off course on an exploration of the New Guinea coast.

Cooktown received its name when in 1770 Captain Cook beached the *Endeavour* there for repairs after striking a reef. The name stuck even though no settlement was made there until over 50 years afterwards.

The city of Geelong obtained its name from the Aboriginal word "jillong" which was its original name. The word means "place of the native companion".

There are some odd names in Australia but not many named after a disease. The Ophthalmia Range in Western Australia was so named by the explorer Ernest Giles because he was suffering continually from that complaint.

Sometimes trains have unusual names because of their history. Two trains which run between Sydney and the Blue Mountains each day are called the *Fish* and the *Chips*. The *Fish* was so-called because the name of its first driver was John Heron, which the educated people thought was "herring". The later train was naturally called the *Chips*.

The *Ghan* train which ran from Marree to Alice Springs obtained its name from the fact that it followed the tracks of the

Afghan camel drivers who provided the transport before the railway was built in 1929.

Castlemaine (Vic.) was originally called Forest Creek, then renamed after Viscount Castlemaine. The Castlemaine beer produced in Queensland is named after the town, but the Fitzgerald family moved their brewery to Brisbane in the late 19th century.

After the first World War many German place names given by German pioneers or explorers were removed and replaced by what were considered more acceptable names. In New South Wales, Germanton became Holbrook, German Creek became Empire Vale. Queensland changed Bergen to Murra Murra, Bismarck to Maclagan, Gehrkevale to Mount Mort, Gramzon to Carbrook, Hapsburg to Kowli, and Murden to Frenchton. In Victoria, Mount Bismarck was changed to Mount Kitchener, Hochkirch to Tarrington, Germantown to Grovedale. In South Australia many of the place names in the Adelaide Hills and Barossa Valley were changed, but some returned to their original names later. Altogether over a hundred names were changed to de-Germanise them. Many people wanted to change the name of Tanunda, but it is an Aboriginal word meaning "wild fowl at creek".

Faulconbridge in the Blue Mountains is named after the mother of five times premier of New South Wales, Sir Henry Parkes. She was born Martha Faulconbridge. Parkes is buried in the town's cemetery.

Alice Springs (N.T.) was named after Alice Gillam Todd (1826-1910). She was wife of the South Australian postmaster-general, Sir Charles Todd, after whom the Todd River is named. Their connection with central Australia arose out of the construction of the Overland Telegraph Line which Todd supervised.

A third of the place names in Australia are Aboriginal in origin. The rest are largely copied from other countries.

The Blue Mountains near Sydney obtained their name from public usage, not as an official title. Governor Phillip called the northern part the Carmarthen Hills, and the southern part the Landsdowne Hills, but the people of Sydney still referred to them as the Blue Mountains because of their characteristic blue haze. Eventually the common name was officially recognised.

Bendigo (Vic.) was supposed to be known as Sandhurst. Abednego William Thompson (1811-1880) was a famous English prize fighter, a hero of the miners on the goldfields. They named the settlement after him and Abednego was corrupted to Bendigo. All attempts to use the official name of Sandhurst failed.

Darwin was named in 1839 by John Lort Stokes, a personal friend of the great naturalist Charles Darwin. The settlement was not founded, however, until 1869. The official name of the new settlement was Palmerston, after the British prime minister, but locals continued to use the original name of Port Darwin. It became official in 1911.

Perth (W.A.) is the only Australian capital city named after a city in another country. It was named in 1829 after Perth in Scotland, probably at the suggestion of the governor, James Stirling, who was Scottish. Perth was selected because the Colonial Secretary at the time, Sir George Murray, was the member of parliament for that city.

NAMES

Australia's international airline QANTAS received its name from the initial letters of the Queensland and Northern Territory Aerial Services from which it developed. It was founded as a local air service for western Queensland in 1920 but has been government-owned since 1947.

The name "Van Diemen's Land" was originally given to Tasmania by Abel Tasman in 1642 in honour of the Dutch governor-general of the East Indies. Later the name was changed to Tasmania in honour of Tasman himself.

Hobart was named after Lord Hobart, secretary of state for the colonies in the British Government at the time that the city was founded, in 1804.

Not all nicknames come from the distant past. In the 1960s the stretch of the Princes Highway from Sale to Bairnsdale (Vic.) was notorious for the loose stones which flew up, smashing car windscreens. Hence its name — "The Crystal Highway".

The Holden motor car got its name from the Holden motor-body building business founded by Edward Wheewall Holden in Adelaide in 1917. In 1930 Holden's merged with General Motors (Australia) to form General Motors-Holden's, but they built only bodies onto American engines and chassis. The first Holden motor car was the FX model, produced in 1948.

There is nothing exotic about the name of Albury (N.S.W.). It is simply the name of a small English village which was fondly remembered by an early settler. Its old English meaning is "the old fort".

Sydney was named after the British home secretary, Lord Sydney, who was largely responsible for the voyage of the First Fleet in 1787.

Cairns in north Queensland was named after Sir William Wellington Cairns, governor of Queensland from 1875 to 1877.

Sydney's King's Cross was formerly called Queen's Cross but the name was changed after Queen Victoria died. By the same reasoning it should have returned to Queen's Cross in 1952 — but it did not.

Visitors to Perth will notice the frequency with which the name "Parmelia" is used, by a major hotel, for example. *Parmelia* was the name of the ship used by their first settlers from England in 1829.

Broken Hill (N.S.W.) was named by the explorer Charles Sturt who almost died from thirst there in 1844. He referred to the hump-backed range of hills as "the broken hill".

Although the name "Australia" is supposed to have been first coined by Matthew Flinders (1774–1814), the name Terra Australis was used on a world chart produced in 1569 by the Flemish geographer Gerhardus Mercator. The name "Australia" was first used by Alexander Dalrymple in his collection of *Voyages of the South Seas* in 1770.

Rockhampton (Qld) was named in 1857 by Land Commissioner W. H. Wiseman. He combined a reference to a chain of rocks in the Fitzroy River nearby, with the name of his home town of Hampton in England.

Queensland's main inland city, Toowoomba, was originally known as "The Swamps". The name is thought to have derived from "twamba", which was

the closest the local Aborigines could get to saying "swamp".

The Isa in Mount Isa (Qld) was the sister of John Campbell Miles who discovered the large silver and lead deposits there in 1923. He named one of the leases Mount Isa after his sister Isabelle, and the name transferred to the town.

There are two Maryboroughs in Australia, named for different reasons. The Maryborough in Queensland was named for Mary Fitzroy, the wife of Governor Fitzroy. The place in Victoria was named after the Irish birthplace of Police Commissioner Daly who formed a police camp there on the goldfields in 1854. Its previous name was Simpson's.

Mount Gambier (S.A.) was the first part of South Australia to be named. It was sighted by Lieutenant James Grant in the *Lady Nelson* in 1800, and named after Admiral Lord Gambier under whom he had served.

Mount Wellington, the spectacular backdrop to Hobart (Tas.), has had many names. Called Pooranetteri and Unghanyahletta by the Aborigines, it was first sighted by Europeans in 1792 by French explorer D'Entrecasteaux who called it Montagne du Plateau; then by Commodore Hayes (1793) who called it Skiddaw; and by Matthew Flinders who called it Mt Table in 1798. Governor Sorell gave it its present name in 1820, after the British military hero of the time.

Narrabeen was an Aboriginal girl who was friendly with the family of a soldier who lived at what is now Narrabeen Lakes. When bushrangers led by Big Mack attacked the Reynolds family in 1836, Narrabeen ran to Parramatta for assistance. Although the Reynolds family were all killed, the soldiers who returned with her killed the bushrangers. The heroism of the young Aboriginal girl was applauded by the people of Sydney and the local lakes and beaches were named after her.

Rottnest Island (W.A.) got its name because Dutch navigator Willem de Vlamingh thought that the quokkas which inhabit the island were giant rats.

People

Edward Gibbon Wakefield (1796-1862), the great colonial reformer who fought to end transportation of convicts to Australia, had been a convict himself. In 1827 he was convicted of persuading a young heiress to elope with him and was held for three years in Newgate prison. Although his theories were tried with little success in South Australia, they were successful in New Zealand.

James Cowley Morgan Fisher was known as the "Nunawading Messiah". In the 1860s his followers believed that he was the Messiah. A man of striking appearance, he once took his followers to Blackburn Lake (Vic.) to pray in the open air while he demonstrated a miracle. "Do ye believe my friends that with the help of your faith I can walk upon water?" he roared from the edge of the lake. "Hallelujah, we believe," they cried. "Well," Fisher replied, raising his eyes to the heavens, "then there is no need for me to do it."

Viscount Montgomery of Alamein was educated for part of his childhood in Hobart (Tas.). His father was the Anglican bishop of Tasmania at the time.

Despite the accolades received by Captain Cook as the discoverer of Australia, his achievement was to have charted the east coast for the first time. Many people had visited the north and west coasts hundreds of years earlier and the Portuguese had made several voyages down the east coast. Cook did not particularly like Australia and never returned after his only visit of 1770.

The movie star Errol Flynn (1909-1959) was born in Hobart (Tas.). He worked as an island trader and gold prospector in New Guinea before going to England in 1934 where he began his acting career. In 1936 he went to the United States and became one of the world's leading movie stars.

Lawrence Hargrave (1850-1915), the Australian pioneer of aviation, built a variety of aircraft and kites. In 1890 he built a plane which was propelled by compressed air and by flapping its wings. It flew for 368 feet (110 metres). It is now in the Museum of Applied Arts and Sciences in Sydney.

Australia had its own Pony Express. When overland mails began between Melbourne and Sydney in 1838, John Bourke carried the mail in a pouch to Sydney. The service lasted for several years with Bourke facing many dangers on every trip. He retired in 1883 and lived to be 88 years of age.

Quong Tart (1850-1903) was a Chinese immigrant gold miner. He came to Australia on a Scottish ship and worked among the Scottish miners at Braidwood (N.S.W.). Quong became an expert on Scottish history, folklore and literature and spoke with a heavy Scottish accent. He attended all of the Scottish gatherings and competed in the Caledonian games, complete with kilt and sporran. "Ma name's MacTart", he would tell astonished onlookers.

When Frederick Bayley Deeming was charged with murder in Windsor (Vic.) in 1891 he claimed that he was the real "Jack the Ripper" of London notoriety. It may never be known whether he was telling the truth or simply trying to escape death on the grounds of insanity. If it was the latter tactic, it was unsuccessful.

Joseph Hawdon (1813-1871) was a pioneer settler who made the first cattle drive from New South Wales to Adelaide. He also made several drives to Victoria. Hawdon settled in Heidelberg (Vic.) and built the Banyule homestead which now houses the Banyule gallery branch of the National Gallery of Victoria. He later migrated to New Zealand.

John Gould, after whom the Gould League of Birdlovers is called, amassed a fortune from making the world bird-conscious. His studies of Australian birds made him world famous. He ate birds, he sold their skins, skeletons, feathers and eggs and even pickled them in their plumage. He wrote *Birds of Australia* and started the craze for stuffed birds in glass cages. All in all he must have destroyed hundreds of birds.

Adam Lindsay Gordon, the poet, is reputed to be one of the greatest horsemen ever. He was playing follow-the-leader on horseback with friends around the Blue Lake at Mount Gambier (S.A.) when he suddenly spurred the horse towards a post-and-rail wooden fence beyond which was a ledge only 2 metres (7 feet) wide. Beyond that was a vertical drop of over 105 metres (350 feet). The horse cleared the rail, twisted in mid-air and landed on the ledge only centimetres from the edge. The famous horseman Lance Skuthorpe later repeated the feat for a bet but nobody else has ever attempted it.

William Dampier (1652-1715), British pirate, adventurer, and explorer, visited Australia's western coast in 1699, over 70 years earlier than Cook's visit to the east coast. The waters around Broome (W.A.) are said to be haunted by the ghost of Dampier's ship, the *Roebuck*.

The old advertisements for Pelaco shirts feature a beaming Aboriginal saying "Mine tinkit they fit". The model for the advertisements was Mulga Fred who came from the Horsham (Vic.) area. He lived to be 85 years of age and died when he was run over by a train in 1949.

Andrew Barton Paterson who wrote "The Man from Snowy River" and "Clancy of the Overflow" used the pseudonym "Banjo" for the first ballads he wrote for the *Bulletin* in the 1890s. Although he had created it himself, it stuck as a nickname.

PEOPLE

Captain Cook was not the first person in his party to set foot on Australian soil. His wife's nephew Isaac Smith, who was one of his boatmen, jumped ashore first on Cook's orders. (Later in life Smith became an Admiral.) Thus the Smiths were among the first Europeans to set foot in Australia, as well as being the most numerous of Australians.

Peter Lalor, leader of the miners at the Eureka Stockade, was wounded in the battle and hunted by the police. Subsequently he was pardoned and was elected to the Victorian Parliament in 1855. His brother James Fintan Lalor was a famous Irish patriot.

A sleeveless shirt or singlet is still sometimes called a Jacky Howe. Howe (1855–1922) was recognised as the world's greatest blade shearer who once sheared 327 ewes in seven hours and 20 minutes without a machine. When machines were introduced in 1904 he used one to shear 337 sheep in an eight-hour day.

When Sir Thomas Blamey (1884–1951) retired from the army in 1945, he became head of a paramilitary force which called itself the Association for the White Army. It claimed to have 100,000 members who were all ex-servicemen and its stated aim was to save Australia from a Communist takeover.

Robert Towns, whose name is remembered in the city of Townsville (Qld) was a "blackbirder" who raided the Pacific Islands for native labourers who were used as virtual slaves in the sugarcane fields. Over 60,000 were brought to Australia before "blackbirding" was abolished in 1904. They were not allowed to settle in Australia but were returned, mostly penniless, to the islands.

William Morris Hughes (1864–1952) was prime minister of Australia from October 1915 to February 1923. In his tempestuous career he had more than 100 private secretaries. Some lasted less than an hour in the job.

To the rest of the world the epitome of the Australian bushman was Chips Rafferty (real name John William Pilbeam Goffage). Chips was born at Broken Hill (N.S.W.) and made films from 1938 to 1970. He died in 1971.

Sir Macpherson Robertson, who founded the MacRobertson chocolate company (now part of Cadbury's), was a great public benefactor. In 1934 he gave £100,000 to the Victorian centenary celebrations. The money was used to finance a Centenary Air Race from London to Melbourne and to build the girls' high school in South Melbourne now named after him, a bridge over the Yarra from Burnley to Toorak and an ornamental fountain in the Domain. Earlier he had financed Antarctic expeditions, and Mawson named MacRobertson Land in Antarctica after him.

Henry James O'Farrell who tried to assassinate Alfred, Duke of Edinburgh, in Sydney in 1868 had Irishman's luck. He might have succeeded if he had not hit the Duke in the metal part of his braces. His failure was complete when he was hanged six months later.

Although explorer John King was rescued by Alfred Howitt after the tragic Burke and Wills expedition, he was in poor health and never really recovered. He died from tuberculosis a few years later at the age of only 31.

The founder of the Myer Emporium, Sidney Myer (real name Simcha Baevski) was born in Russia and arrived

in Australia penniless. He worked as a wrapper in an underclothing factory while he learned English, then sold the products from a horse and cart in the country. In 1900 he opened a small drapery shop in Bendigo before buying an existing drapery shop in Bourke Street, Melbourne, in 1911. These days the Myer group has over 150 retail outlets in Australia. The Bourke Street shop has grown into a huge multi-storey store which is the biggest shop in the world, outside the U.S.A. In 1985 the company merged with G. J. Coles and Co. Ltd to make the biggest retail company in Australia. Over 20 per cent of all retail sales in Australia are made through the Coles-Myer group.

Herbert Hoover, president of the United States from 1929 to 1933, spent several years in Australia. Between 1897 and 1907 he managed mines in Western Australia and worked in the Broken Hill mines.

A major critic of the Gallipoli campaign in 1915 was Keith Murdoch, later to be knighted. He visited the war zone and despite threats from the British commanders he criticised them and the impossibility of the campaign. After the war he became editor of Melbourne's *Herald* and later the managing-director of the Herald-Weekly Times group. During the second World War he was director-general of information for the Federal Government. He was of course the father of Rupert Murdoch, newspaper owner and well-known international businessman.

The Arctic explorer, Sir John Franklin, was lieutenant-governor of Van Diemen's Land from 1837 to 1843. He was recalled in 1843 after accusations that his wife had too much influence in government affairs. He died on another Arctic expedition in 1847. His wife spent many years and a great amount of money trying to find out what happened to him.

Although Francis Forde was prime minister of Australia for only a week in 1945, between the death of Curtin and the election of Chifley, he continued to receive all the comforts of an ex-prime minister for the rest of his life. He had a secretarial assistant and chauffeured car at the taxpayer's expense until he died over 30 years later.

Robert O'Hara Burke, the explorer, certainly got around. He was born in Ireland, became a cadet in the Hungarian Hussars, then a policeman back in Ireland. In 1852 he migrated to Van Diemen's Land, then moved to Victoria where he became a police inspector. He went back to Ireland to enlist for the Crimean War but arrived after it had finished. So he returned to Victoria and re-entered the police force. The rest is in the history books.

Henry Higgins, president of the Arbitration Court, whose Harvester Judgement established the principle of a basic wage was a politician in both the Victorian Parliament (where he lost his seat because of his opposition to the Boer War) and of the Federal Parliament. He left Parliament to join the High Court in 1906.

Sir Charles Moses was general manager of the A.B.C. from 1935 to 1965 and is famous for his part in the early "fake" test cricket broadcasts. He has held many public offices and has been president of the Amateur Athletic Association. In his youth he was the heavyweight boxing champion of Victoria and also Victorian discus champion.

PEOPLE

Sir Thomas Brisbane, governor of New South Wales (1821-1825), was a well-known astronomer in Europe. While in Australia he mapped over 7000 of the stars in the southern skies. He was Australia's first significant astronomer.

Explorers Hume and Hovell, who made an epic overland journey in 1824 from Sydney to Gunning (N.S.W.) then to Geelong (Vic.), often argued during their journey. In 1853 they became open enemies when Hume misinterpreted a speech by Hovell at Geelong as a claim to having discovered the site of Geelong alone. They remained enemies, often attacking one another in letters to the newspapers. In actual fact, when they discovered the site of Geelong both of them thought that they had reached Westernport Bay.

Charles Rasp was a German migrant who arrived in Victoria in 1869. He worked as a boundary rider at Mt Gipps station in the Barrier Range (N.S.W.) where in 1883 he discovered what he thought was a "mountain of tin". It turned out to be silver and lead, and he formed a syndicate. In 1885 they launched a public company to raise capital. Rasp bought out one of the other syndicate members for only £10. The company they launched was Broken Hill Proprietary Co. Ltd (B.H.P.) — now Australia's biggest company, "the big Australian".

Captain James Cook was one of the greatest British seamen. His father did not want him to be a sailor and he was apprenticed to a grocer and then a haberdasher before going to sea.

One of the great triers was Arthur Orton, a butcher from Wagga Wagga. Reading about the disappearance of Lady Tichborne's son in England, he went to England and claimed to be her missing son and heir. For some time he was believed, and even when his dishonesty was exposed Lady Tichborne still believed in him.

John Harrison, the great goldfields reformer, was known as "the digger's champion". He lobbied Governor LaTrobe and made public speeches in support of the Eureka rebels. His son Henry first codified the rules for Australian Rules football.

Herbert Vere Evatt (1894-1965) was leader of the Australian Labor Party from 1951 to 1960. However, before this he was president of the General Assembly of the United Nations in 1948 and 1949.

CAPTAIN COOK DISCOVERS THE BLUEBOTTLE

PEOPLE

Although there are always difficulties in measuring such things, Reginald Beck of Sydney appears to have been the longest-living Australian. He was born in 1817, when Napoleon was still alive and the first bank opened in the Sydney settlement, and died in 1928 when the first links with the rest of the world by aeroplane were being created—he was 111 years of age.

William James Farrer (1845–1906) developed the rust-free wheat strains that revolutionised the wheat industry late last century. He worked for many years as a contract surveyor before resigning to develop new strains of wheat. He worked for 20 years at this task and was still researching when he died of heart disease.

The actor Jack Thompson (born 1940) whose presence seems inevitable in any epic Australian movie was born John Payne.

Sir Sidney Kidman (1857–1935) was the first person to make a success of farming in the inland. He started at 13 years of age by buying a one-eyed horse for 5/- and went on to become a knight, a millionaire and owner of nearly 300,000 square kilometres (116,000 square miles) of land. He was notorious for his meanness and even today in the outback, golden syrup is sometimes referred to as "Kidman's blood mixture" or "Kidman's joy".

Sir John Monash (1865–1931), after whom Melbourne's second university is named, is best known as a soldier. However, before he joined the army he was an engineer who pioneered construction in reinforced concrete. After the war he became general manager of the State Electricity Commission of Victoria and was largely responsible for development of Victoria's brown coal deposits in the Latrobe Valley.

The great poet Henry Lawson (1867–1922) was totally deaf from the age of 14. Originally an apprentice coach-painter, he wrote stories and poetry part-time, until he became well known. By the age of 40 he was an alcoholic, and this hastened his premature death.

It is often argued, not without reason, that Lachlan Macquarie, who was governor of New South Wales from 1809 to 1821, was the best of the early governors. He was certainly greatly mourned when he died in England three years after leaving Sydney. Notwithstanding that fact there was no monument erected to him until 1973.

William Charles Wentworth (1793–1872) was the first Australian-born holder of an important office. He was appointed provost-marshal in 1811 when he was only 18 years of age. In 1813 when he was only 19 years of age he crossed the Blue Mountains with Blaxland and Lawson. This was only the start of a life of achievement.

William John Turner Clarke (1801–1874) founder of the titled Clarke family, bastions of Australian society, was a London-born butcher who survived the 1840s Depression by buying sheep and boiling them down for tallow which was exported to England. Clarke used the profits to buy land and when he died left an estate of 90,000 hectares (225,000 acres) and £2.5 million.

John Fairfax, founder of the Fairfax newspaper empire, started as an apprentice printer and binder at the age of 11. He was driven bankrupt in England due to the expenses of a libel

action he successfully defended, and moved to Sydney in 1838. Fairfax worked as a compositor and a librarian before buying the *Sydney Morning Herald* in 1841, largely financed by David Jones, the founder of the store. In 1851, 15 years after his bankruptcy, he returned to England to pay off all of his debts.

The actress Mia Farrow, who once married Frank Sinatra, has an Australian father. John Farrow was a film director and author, born in Sydney, who went to Hollywood in the 1930s and produced, directed and wrote film scripts. He won an Oscar in 1956 for the screenplay of *Around the World in 80 Days*. Mia's mother is the actress Maureen O'Sullivan.

Daniel Bunce (1813-1872) does not rate much of a mention as an historical figure but he was very much on the fringes of great events. He migrated to Hobart in 1835 and started Tasmania's first plant nursery before crossing to Melbourne. He was the first European to climb the Dandenong Ranges and married the daughter of John Batman, Melbourne's founder. He spent the last 15 years of his life quietly as director of the Geelong Botanical Gardens.

Abel Tasman, who first explored the water around Australia, had the reputation of being a vicious master. He carried large crews because so many died from disease and maltreatment. The life expectancy of his crew members was below 30 years of age. His crews were recruited from slum areas, largely by press gangs.

In 1649 Tasman returned to his ship much the worse for drink. He accused two sailors of disobeying his command and ordered other sailors to hang one for his disobedience. When almost strangled, the sailor was dropped to the ground. Tasman was suspended by the East India Company for two years as a punishment.

Sir Joseph Banks (1743-1820) deserves to be regarded as the "father of Australia" because it was he rather than Cook who continually urged the British Government to establish a convict settlement in Australia. Eventually they agreed and he acted as a consultant to the First Fleet and the early settlement.

Sir Charles Kingsford Smith (1897-1935), Australia's best-known pioneer aviator, always walked with a limp. This was the result of losing two toes and part of his foot when shot down by the Germans in the first World War. In 1919 Kingsford Smith tried to enter the Britain-Australia air race but was rejected because he could not navigate.

D'Arcy Wentworth (1762-1827), founder of the Wentworth political dynasty, decided to migrate to Sydney in 1790 after being acquitted for the third time of charges of highway robbery. He practised medicine at Norfolk Island and in Sydney and received grants of land.

Sir Henry Parkes (1815-1896), who was one of the fathers of Federation, had little education. At eight years of age he was put to work in the ivory trade and migrated to Australia in 1839 where he set up in Sydney as an ivory dealer. He later entered parliament and served five terms as premier of New South Wales.

Sir Charles Hotham who was governor of Victoria in 1854-1855 must rate as one of the most disliked vice-regal personages of all time, mainly because he was so miserly. Although he received an immense salary and living

allowance, he kept his own pigs, cows and chickens in the grounds of Government House and sold eggs and butter to supplement his income. The Melbourne *Punch* referred to him as "His Eggsellency".

Jorgen Jorgensen (1780–1841) was a Danish adventurer who first visited Australia in 1800. In 1809 he took a merchant ship to Iceland and arrested the Danish governor. He then sent a message to London that he had annexed Iceland to Britain; meanwhile he ruled as self-appointed king. The British Government refused to accept Iceland and sent a naval vessel to arrest him and restore Danish rule. In 1820 he was sentenced to transportation for life for petty crime and landed in Tasmania in 1826. He was pardoned, became a constable and was later editor of a local newspaper.

Francis Greenway whose countenance is featured on the front of the $10 note, nearly did not appear there. In 1812 he received a death sentence for forging a contract document. Fortunately this was commuted to life imprisonment and he was transported to New South Wales. He was Australia's first architect and he designed many of Sydney's oldest buildings.

George (Chinese) Morrison (1862–1920) was probably the greatest expert on China ever, and was known as the "uncrowned King of China". Even as a boy it was obvious he was going to go a long way In 1877, at 15, he walked from Geelong (Vic.) to Adelaide and in 1879 walked from the Gulf of Carpentaria (Qld) to Geelong in 123 days, a journey of 3300 kilometres (2046 miles) through largely unexplored territory. His son Bill Morrison was a Cabinet minister in the Whitlam Labor Government.

John Macarthur (1767–1834), the pioneer farmer and soldier, was a great opportunist. In 1801 Macarthur wounded an opponent in an illegal duel. Governor Philip Gidley King sent him to England for trial before a military tribunal. The trial never took place but Macarthur took the opportunity to show sample fleece to British wool merchants. He resigned from the army and returned to the colony to develop the wool industry. He carried with him a letter from the British Government suggesting that he be granted 5000 acres (2000 hectares) of the best land in the colony, with another 5000 acres if he successfully developed the industry. He even obtained some rare merino sheep from George III's own flocks.

Blind Freddy really existed. In the 1920s there was a blind hawker who sold matches and pencils around the streets of Sydney. His name was Freddy and his blindness never seemed to hamper his mobility; the saying grew— "even Blind Freddy could see that".

William Buckley (1780–1856) was a convict who escaped from the unsuccessful settlement near Sorrento (Vic.) in 1803. Thirty-two years later he was found by John Batman, living with Aborigines. In 1837 he went to live in Tasmania, where he married and worked as a gatekeeper.

Two of the sons of the novelist Charles Dickens lived in Australia. Edward Dickens managed a station in New South Wales, married a squatter's daughter, but went bankrupt when he took over his own station. Alfred Dickens was a stock and station agent at Hamilton in Victoria and still has descendants in the area.

Places

Most Australians know that Captain Cook's cottage is preserved in Melbourne's Fitzroy Gardens. Unfortunately there is no evidence that Captain Cook ever lived in it, or even stopped in it. It was brought from Great Ayton in Yorkshire as a part of the Victorian centenary celebrations in 1934. It was built by Cook's father well after Cook had left home and apparently Cook only visited him once after it was built. This was in 1771, after he had explored the Australian east coast.

A country mansion in Central Tasmania called Mona Vale is often referred to as "Calendar House" because it has 365 windows, 52 rooms, 12 chimneys and 7 entrances. It was completed in 1868.

Although Broken Hill is in New South Wales it does most of its business with Adelaide, rather than Sydney, because Adelaide is closer. As a result it is the only city in New South Wales to use South Australian time.

The public memorial hall to the cactoblastis insect, which was introduced from South America to destroy over 24 million hectares (60 million acres) of prickly-pear plants, stands at Boonarga (Qld). It is the only public memorial to an insect, anywhere in the world.

The oldest building in Western Australia is the so-called Round House at the bottom end of High Street, Fremantle. It is actually not round at all, but 12-sided. It was built by H. W. Revely in 1831 as a gaol but proved much too small for this purpose once transportation was introduced. It is preserved as an historic monument.

The Workingman's Club in Mildura (Vic.) is supposed to have the longest continuous bar in the world.

Bennelong Point on Sydney Harbour has had an interesting history. It was the location where cattle were kept by the First Fleet, then, the location of the Aboriginal Bennelong's hut. In 1821 a

fort was constructed there and named Fort Macquarie. This was demolished in 1902 and a tram depot built in its place. Nowadays it is the site of the Sydney Opera House.

Every town of any size in Australia has a "Mechanics Institute" or "Mechanics Hall". These were set up in accordance with the ideas of George Birkbeck, an English teacher. They were designed to be places where tradesmen could read and attend lectures and were important sources of adult education. The first ones in Australia were set up in Sydney in 1833 and Melbourne in 1839. Often in New South Wales they are known as "Schools of Art".

Melbourne's Exhibition Building has had a chequered history. It was built for the great 1880 Exhibition. In 1901 it acted as the first Commonwealth Parliament House, but it was also used as a hospital in the 1919 influenza epidemic, as Victoria's Parliament House in 1927 and for a grand Christmas party for 11,500 unemployed during the Great Depression. It was the venue for some sporting events at the 1956 Olympics. When it was built it was the biggest building in Australia.

The point where Queensland, South Australia and the Northern Territory meet is referred to as Poeppel's Corner. Augustus Poeppel was the South Australian Government surveyor who surveyed the South Australia—Queensland border. The hardwood peg he used to mark the "corner" has since been replaced by a concrete one.

South Australia is the only State with common boundaries with all of the other mainland States.

The mineral springs at Daylesford (Vic.) produce a large part of the mineral water sold in Australia. The Central Spring in Daylesford produces 135,000 litres (about 30,000 gallons) of water a day. The Victorian Government is to undertake a programme to promote the area as a tourist centre.

In Hobart (Tas.) there is an arcade called the Cat and Fiddle Arcade. In its central square is a clock which acts out the "Hi-Diddle-Diddle" nursery rhyme every hour. The cat plays the fiddle, the cow jumps over the moon and the dish runs away with the spoon. The arcade was named after an old inn which stood on the site originally.

The oldest building still standing in Sydney is John Cadman's Cottage. John Cadman was transported to Sydney in 1798 and later became superintendent of government boats at the dockyard. It is classified by the National Trust and has been restored as part of the Sydney Cove Maritime Museum.

The Australian War Memorial in Canberra claims to be Australia's most visited tourist attraction. It contains paintings, relics, sculptures, scale models and dioramas relating to all wars in which Australians have fought. It contains over 70,000 books and a vast collection of newspaper articles, photographs, posters, postage stamps and war memorabilia. The remains of one of the miniature submarines that attacked Sydney Harbour is displayed in the grounds.

The town of Bombala in southern New South Wales used to be known as the "town of women" because in summer many of the men would leave to take the cattle to higher pastures, not returning until the winter. It was one of the popular choices for federal capital before Canberra was selected.

PLACES  93

There is a little bit of Australia in the Strand, London. Australia House was set up in 1918. It acts as a focal point for Australians in England, with Australian newspapers readily available.

The Australian-American War Memorial in Canberra is 48 metres (150 feet) high and is sheathed in sand-blasted aluminium. The column is surmounted by an eagle. The memorial commemorates the help given by the United States to Australia in the second World War. It was unveiled in 1954.

King Island is the biggest island in Bass Strait. It is about half way between Victoria and Tasmania and was notorious for shipwrecks in the 19th century. Scheelite mining is its major industry. Fishing, farming and tourism are also important.

In the 1820s Kangaroo Island (S.A.) was a sealing and whaling settlement. So wild was the settlement of runaway convicts, part-Aborigines and bad types that warships were sent from Sydney to overthrow the settlement and its inhabitants.

Kalgoorlie (W.A.) gets its water supply from the Mundaring Reservoir near Perth, 560 kilometes (347 miles) away. It takes the water about a month to make the journey. The pipeline was opened in 1903.

Fort Denison in Sydney Harbour was originally a small rocky peak about 10 metres (30 feet) high. It was cut back to high water level and a fort was constructed in 1857. Fear of a Russian invasion led to construction of the tower, and guns were mounted.

The highest permanent township in Australia is Kiandra (N.S.W.) which is 1414 metres (4640 feet) above sea level.

The tallest man-made structure in Australia is the radio tower, "Tower Zero" at the U.S. Navy Communications Centre at North-West Cape (W.A.). It is 387 metres (1271 feet) high.

The highest church spire in Australia is that of St Patrick's Cathedral in Melbourne. It is 103.6 metres (340 feet) high.

The Australian Capital Territory was divided from New South Wales as a separate territory in 1911, and the future capital was named Canberra in 1913.

The Tank Stream which provided Sydney's first water supply when the first settlement began is now a stormwater drain 6 metres (20 feet) under the city's streets. It enters Circular Quay at the western end of the ferry terminals.

There are lead-shot towers still standing in Sydney and Melbourne and a famous one at Taroona near Hobart (Tas.). Molten lead was poured into a colander which it dripped through, then fell the 50 metres (150 feet) or so into cooling water at the bottom. The lead shot was then used in shotgun cartridges.

If you look at a map of Australia, Bourke (N.S.W.) looks an unlikely place for a shipping casualty. Bourke is on the Darling River and in 1926 the Murray River steamer *Nile* was destroyed there by fire some 2400 kilometres (1488 miles) from its home port of Goolwa (S.A.) on the Murray. The remains of the steamer are still there somewhere on the river bed.

The Hutt River Province in Western Australia is a "principality" which has seceded from Western Australia. Leonard George Casley, a farmer, declared his property a separate sovereign state and called himself "Prince Leonard" after a dispute with the Western Australian Government over his wheat quota. The province is not officially recognised by other governments in Australia but is recognised by several countries overseas. It issues its own postage stamps and money and Prince Leonard travels overseas on a Hutt Province passport, without being questioned about its validity.

During a severe storm at Bondi in July 1912 a huge rock weighing more than 235 tonnes (240 tons) was thrown up from the sea on to Ben Buckler, the headland on the northern side of the beach.

In South Australia's Barossa Valley the German tradition is very obvious. The original German settlers, 537 Lutherans who were suffering religious persecution in Prussia, were settled on land owned by George Fife Angas in 1838. These days German scholars visit the Barossa Valley to observe the traditions of German life preserved from 150 years ago.

Many of the permanent residents on Norfolk Island, an Australian territory 1400 kilometres (908 miles) north-east of Sydney, are descendants of the *Bounty* mutineers who moved there from Pitcairn Island in 1856.

Victoria, which now refers to itself as "The Garden State", was referred to by first World War diggers as the Cabbage Patch, or Cabbage Garden. A Victorian was a cabbage-lander or cabbage-patcher.

The Black Stump was a real place. It was a wine shanty near Coolah (N.S.W.) on the Gunnedah road. It closed down in the 1890s and was eventually destroyed by fire.

Although the first permanent settlement in New South Wales was moved from Botany Bay to Sydney Cove within a week, the name Botany Bay was still sometimes used to describe the whole colony, even in the 19th century.

Boyd Town on Twofold Bay (N.S.W.) now lies in ruins. It was built by Benjamin Boyd, a Scotsman, in the 1840s. At one stage it possessed a lighthouse, a 100-metre-long jetty, an imitation Gothic church, solid brick houses and an Elizabethan-style inn.

PLACES

Boyd disappeared in the Solomon Islands in 1851.

The old rabbitproof fence was built from Eucla in Western Australia to Queensland. It was nearly 10,000 kilometres (6200 miles) long but is now in disrepair. It is still the longest fence in the world.

Bandywallop is a mythical country settlement. So also are Woop Woop and Snake Gully (although there is a Snake Valley near Ballarat, Victoria).

Mount Morgan (Qld), where the miners were a wild bunch, was known as the town of the four G's — girls, goats, galahs and glass bottles.

In the grounds of Melbourne's Exhibition Building there is a roughly shaped pillar of sandstone without any identifying inscription. It was placed there in 1878 by the member for Stawell in the Victorian Legislative Assembly as a sample of Stawell sandstone, which he wanted to be used as the building material for the Exhibition Building. When it was decided to use another material he refused to remove it, and it has remained there ever since.

At Federation in 1910 Victoria's choice for national capital was Albury on the Victoria-New South Wales border. In 1904 the Federal Parliament decided that it would be near Dalgety in the far south-east of New South Wales, but the New South Wales Government would not agree. Finally the site at Canberra was agreed upon as a compromise and building commenced in 1913.

The site on which the Queensland capital, Brisbane, stands was surveyed by John Oxley in 1823. It was originally called Moreton Bay but it was renamed after Sir Thomas Brisbane who was then governor of New South Wales. It was originally a penal settlement but the convicts were removed in 1839. Queensland was a part of New South Wales until 1859 when it became a separate colony.

Ballarat is the largest inland city in Victoria. The official spelling is Ballaarat but nobody outside the city seems to bother with the extra "a".

Australia comprises six States and two mainland Territories plus external Territories which are often forgotten. The external territories are the Ashmore and Cartier Islands, the Australian Antarctic Territory, Christmas Island, Cocos Islands, Heard and McDonald Islands and Norfolk Island.

Part of the Australian Capital Territory is nowhere near Canberra. It is on the coast, at Jervis Bay. The bay and the surrounding 73 square kilometres (28 square miles) is used by the Royal Australian Navy and as a port for Canberra. It became part of the Australian Capital Territory in 1915.

From 1875 to 1915, Moonta was the largest town in South Australia outside Adelaide. It was a copper-mining centre populated almost entirely by Cornish families. When the mines closed in 1923 its population declined, but it is now increasing again partly due to tourism.

Politics

Altogether in the 13 Australian State and Federal Houses of Parliament there are 784 members of parliament, which means there is one politician for about every 20,000 people. This makes Australians about the most governed people in the world and costs over $180 million a year.

The Australian Constitution was drafted by conventions in Australia but had to be approved by the British Parliament.
The British wanted four changes made:
(a) They objected to the phrase, "This Act shall bind the Crown".
(b) They wanted a clause removed which gave Australian laws control over British ships sailing from one Australian port to another.
(c) They objected to a clause which would have prevented State and federal cases over Constitutions going to the Privy Council.
(d) They wanted a clause inserted which stated that if British and Australian law conflicted, British law would have precedence.
   The Australian delegation agreed to make the first two changes, came to a compromise on the third, and the fourth remained unresolved.

Sir Robert Menzies was the longest ruling prime minister in Australia. He was prime minister without a break from 1949 to his retirement in 1966.

In 1893 a group of Australians migrated to Paraguay in South America to set up a socialist commune. The leader was William Lane and the group called itself the New Australia Cooperative Settlement Association. After many early squabbles the commune survived but slowly lost its socialist characteristics as it was assimilated into the local population.

The national anthem is still officially "God Save the Queen". It is supposed to be played whenever regal or vice-regal personages are present, at defence forces occasions, and on occasions where the Queen is toasted or singing is appropriate. The national tune, "Advance Australia Fair", is used

POLITICS

for sporting events, the close of television transmission and other occasions when the organisers of the function concerned feel that it is more appropriate. Its words have no official recognition.

Queensland is the only State in Australia without an upper house in its parliament. It was abolished in 1922.

The Australian Labor Party is the oldest political party in Australia. It was founded in 1891. The National Country Party was formed in 1918, and the Liberal Party was not founded until 1944. The Australians Democrats appeared in 1977.

Altogether there have been 16 referendums on 36 different topics since Federation. Only eight of these topics have been carried. The Constitution requires a majority of States (at least four out of six) to agree, and an overall majority of the population must also agree.

In 1925 Thomas Ley was New South Wales minister for Justice. His contestant for the federal seat of Barton in the elections of that year was Frederick McDonald. McDonald disappeared in suspicious circumstances and was never sighted again. Ley was convicted of murder—not McDonald's—in England three years later. He was found guilty but insane and committed to an asylum where he died. McDonald's fate is still unknown.

In 1939 J. N. Lawson was minister for Trade and Customs in the first Menzies Government. He negotiated with Mr W. J. Smith the managing director of A.C.I. to obtain the lease of a racehorse "Billy" in return for A.C.I. obtaining a monopoly to manufacture motor cars. He resigned in 1940 when the details became public.

The shortest serving senator in Australian history is Lionel Thomas Courtenay. His term commenced on 1 July 1935, but he died on 11 July, before the Senate had met. However, he is considered to have been a senator even though he was never sworn in because the writs for the election had been returned before he died.

Our shortest serving prime minister was Frank Forde. He took office on 6 July 1945 and was superseded by Ben Chifley only eight days later.

Because of the large number of its members and higher salaries and allowances, the Queensland Parliament costs more to operate each year than that in Western Australia, even though Queensland has no upper house.

George Reid was prime minister of Australia from 1904 to 1906. He was very fat—and once someone in a crowd called out, "What are you going to call it, George?" "If it's a boy," Reid answered, "I'll call it after myself. If it's a girl I'll call it Victoria after our Queen. But if, as I strongly suspect, it's nothing but piss and wind I'll call it after you, sir."

Australia's youngest prime minister was the Hon. John Watson (1867–1941) who was 37 years and 18 days old when he took office in 1904. He was also the first Labor prime minister, but was in the office for only four months.

Jack Lang, premier of New South Wales during the Depression, liked to be seen as the friend of the poor but it was he who was responsible for the Bloody Friday battle at Newtown, Sydney, in 1931. Encouraged by Lang, the police tried to evict unemployed workers from a barricaded house and 13 police and 14 workers were injured.

POLITICS

Sir Thomas Playford was premier of South Australia from 5 November 1938 to 10 March 1965; a period of 26 years without a break, which is a record for the British Commonwealth. His grandfather was also premier of South Australia in 1887 and 1893.

The Australian Labor Party should by its nature be in favour of the nationalisation of industry. However in 1949 the Chifley Government stated its intention to nationalise the private banks and was decimated in the election which followed. Labor did not regain power for 23 years. Hence the reluctance to even mention it. Most constitutional experts believe it is not possible to nationalise industries in Australia without a referendum.

The first political party in Australia was the "Australian Patriotic Association" formed in 1835 by William Charles Wentworth and others. It lobbied the British Parliament for election of representatives, rather than appointment by the Governor.

It seems strange that there is always so much tension between the Labor Party and the Australian Security Intelligence Organisation (A.S.I.O.), our intelligence organisation. After all, it was created by the Chifley Labor Government in 1949.

Arthur Calwell (1896–1973), who is often described as the architect of Australia's immigration scheme, was a fervent supporter of the white Australia policy right up to his death. In 1947 he endeared himself to all Asians with his comment that "two Wongs do not make a White".

Child endowment or family allowance was introduced by the New South Wales State Government under Jack Lang in 1927. In 1941 the Curtin Labor Government made it a national scheme.

The Commonwealth Police was formed by Prime Minister W. M. Hughes in 1917. A week earlier the Queensland police had refused to prosecute an anti-conscription demonstrator who threw two eggs at Hughes. Without consulting Parliament he used the War Precautions Act to start his own Commonwealth Police Force.

Alfred Deakin (1856–1919), second prime minister of Australia, refused to accept titles which were frequently offered. He started his employment as bookkeeper for Cobb & Co. He was fiercely nationalistic and did not believe that honours should be accepted from Britain.

When the American fleet, referred to as the "Great White Fleet" made a world goodwill tour in 1908, Deakin invited it to visit Australia in defiance of the British Government, which controlled our foreign policy. His reason was to impress the increasingly militant Japanese that Australia could call on powerful friends if attacked.

There was an office of governor-general of Australia before Australia officially existed as a country. Once responsible government was granted to New South Wales in 1855 the governor of New South Wales was also titled governor-general of Australia. The first was Sir William Denison.

The Democratic Labor Party is no longer a force in Australian politics, but from 1956 to 1972 it played a big part in keeping the Australian Labor Party out of federal office by giving its preferences to the Liberal-Country Party coalition. It was an anti-Communist conservative party support-

POLITICS

ed unofficially by the Roman Catholic Church, and at one stage held the balance of power in the Senate, with five senators. It was largely the pressure exerted by the D.L.P. at this stage which led to the introduction of State aid for church-owned schools.

R. J. L. Hawke, the Labor politician and prime minister, was a Rhodes scholar at Oxford from 1953 to 1955. His thesis was about the Australian system of conciliation and arbitration. He later abandoned the doctorate at the Australian National University in Canberra to become research officer for the A.C.T.U., A.C.T.U. advocate, president of the A.C.T.U., president of the Labor Party, then prime minister.

R. G. Menzies was attorney-general of Australia when workers refused to load pig-iron bound for Japan, at Port Kembla in 1938. He used provisions of the Transport Workers Act to force them to load it or be jailed, despite the attacks by Japan on China and the workers' fears that the attacks may spread to other parts of the region, including Australia. From then on, even when he became prime minister, he was referred to as "Pig-Iron Bob". It is quite likely that some of that pig-iron came back to Australia in the bombs dropped on Darwin and other northern towns in 1942.

Most people have seen the old film footage of Captain de Groot on horseback, slashing the ribbon at the opening of the Sydney Harbour Bridge, but it is often not made clear why he did it. He was a member of the New Guard, an extreme right-wing para-military organisation. They were pro-Empire and anti-Communist, and anti-Jack Lang the Labor premier, who was to perform the opening ceremony. After Jack Lang was dismissed, the movement lost its main reason for existence and disintegrated. At one stage in 1931 it is thought to have numbered 50,000 members.

When the Australian Commonwealth was being planned in the 1890s it was hoped that New Zealand would join it, and New Zealand representatives participated in some of the planning conventions. Eventually, however, New Zealand decided to remain independent and became a separate dominion in 1907.

The Australia Party still exists but it is not a political force. It was formed in 1966 as the breakaway Liberal Reform Group opposing Australian involvement in the Vietnam war. It adopted the name Australia Party in 1969 but has never won more than three per cent of the vote in a federal election.

Sir Robert Menzies not only led the Liberal Party from 1944 to 1966, he created it. When the United Australia Party disintegrated in the early 1940s Menzies created the present Liberal Party out of the debris.

Some people who are not interested in politics or who know nothing about the parties, vote by putting their preferences on the voting form in order of the candidates as listed, who are in alphabetical order. The "donkey vote" so recorded can elect a candidate in a marginal seat by giving him up to three per cent extra votes. This leads the lesser political parties to choose candidates with names starting with "A" or "B".

Income tax was originally a State tax. It was introduced by South Australia (1884), Tasmania (1894), Victoria (1895), New South Wales (1895), Queensland (1902) and Western

Australia (1907). In 1915 the Commonwealth introduced it as a temporary wartime measure. After the war both the States and the Commonwealth continued the tax until 1942 when the States agreed to give the Commonwealth the right to collect it exclusively for the duration of the Second World War. After the war the Commonwealth did not relinquish its income tax powers and despite State challenges in the High Court still holds exclusively the power to tax incomes.

The first Commonwealth public servants were members of the Victorian and New South Wales Customs departments who were transferred to Commonwealth control before Federation to dismantle the customs barriers between the colonies. It was 1904 before the Commonwealth Public Service formally came into existence.

In 1934 the people of Western Australia voted two-to-one to break away from the rest of Australia. The State Government took no action, but the matter still raises its head occasionally.

Until the late 1930s Australia had a great reluctance to stand on its own two feet. It was not until this period that we sent our own ambassadors to Japan, China and the United States. Before that we were represented by the British Ambassador and were tied to British policy.

The Australian Constitution allows for the creation of new States. Over the years several groups have tried to achieve separate statehood for their areas. The most persistent have been the New England district of New South Wales, the Riverina district of New South Wales, the Kalgoorlie district of Western Australia, and the northern part of Queensland.

Labor Prime Minister Hawke is not the first politician in his family. His uncle Albert Redvers George Hawke was premier of Western Australia from 1953 to 1959.

The Workers Party is one of the quainter small parties in Australian politics. It is against government control of our lives, and advocates a totally free market economy with no government trading activities, and a great reduction in taxes. All government services including ambulance services, fire brigades, hospitals and education would operate through private enterprise without government funding. So far it has failed to attract a following substantial enough to empower the adoption of its policies.

William Morris Hughes (1862–1952) was prime minister of Australia, leading both opposing political parties in turn. In 1915 he became Labor prime minister but was defeated on the conscription referendum. He was expelled from the Labor Party, joined the Nationalist Opposition and formed a National Party cabinet. In 1917 he tried another referendum on conscription but was defeated again by an increased majority. However, he retained the post of prime minister until 1923 and remained in parliament until 1949.

Shame

In 1927 the Queensland Government declared a one month open season on possums and koalas. The final kill figures were—possums 1,014,632, koalas 584,738. Even today the koala population of Queensland has not completely recovered from this onslaught.

Early punishments were brutal. In 1790 James Barry was given a sentence of 1000 lashes for breaking into a settler's home. He collapsed after 270 of them. On medical advice he took the other 730 lashes in instalments spread over five sessions.

When secondary schooling was expanding in the late 1920s the ruling classes were disturbed that education of the working class might lead to over-education for their place in life. There was a strong movement to reintroduce fees for secondary education to limit the access of the working class.

An intercolonial conference in 1888 agreed that all mainland Australian States would let in only one Chinese person for every 500 tonnes of ship's cargo. This effectively ended Chinese migration.

In the 1890s the mace from the Victorian Legislative Assembly disappeared. A Royal Commission failed to prove anything but it was rumoured that several members (including Tommy Bent, the premier) had held a wild party with wine, women and song, and that the mace was to be seen in one of the local houses of ill fame. It was never found.

The commander of the Australian Eighth Division trapped in Singapore by the Japanese in 1942 was Henry Gordon Bennett. He escaped from Singapore leaving the Eighth Division to fend for itself. A military court of enquiry found that he was not justified in leaving his troops. He resigned from the army but faced no punishment.

In the early years of Victoria even the platypus was hunted for its pelt, and rugs made from up to 60 platypus pelts were highly prized.

In 1860 and 1861 the miners around Young (N.S.W.) attacked the Chinese miners on several occasions. At Lambing Flat on 30 June 1861, 3000

whites marching behind a "No Chinese" banner attacked the Chinese, bashing them and cutting off their pigtails. They plundered their victims' camps and burned the tents and shacks to the ground. The final result was that the New South Wales government restricted Chinese immigration.

In the early days greyhound coursing was quite popular, using wallabies, possums and other inoffensive wildlife as prey. Twenty or 30 animals might be released in an afternoon and torn apart to the cheers of the onlookers.

In the 1860s and 1870s the kangaroo shoot was popular with wealthier people. They would travel to Dromana by steamer arriving just before dawn to be met by stockmen. The guns would be arranged in a semi-circle, each person about 150 metres (500 feet) apart. Cracking stockwhips and yelling, the stockmen would drive the kangaroos towards the guns, helped by dogs. Kangaroos were killed hundreds at a time in this way in the name of sport.

In the second half of the 19th century there was a movement to combat Catholic influence and maintain the Protestant character of Australian society. Sir Henry Parkes was involved with these so-called Protestant Defence Associations, which were afraid of Catholic domination of the Labor movement. In 1902 they organised a protest petition of over 30,000 signatures when Sir Edmund Barton, the prime minister, had an audience with the Pope in Rome.

In 1838 nearly 30 Aboriginal men, women and children were murdered at Myall Creek Station near Narrabri in northern New South Wales. The New South Wales Attorney-General had great trouble in bringing the men responsible to trial. He was criticised for his persistence in the matter by the press and the public generally. Eventually seven men were hanged, but the station owner Henry Danger, who supported the murders, was never charged. The rejection by Governor Gipps of several petitions for mercy was the start of tougher government action on the killing of Aborigines.

In 1923 Melbourne's policemen went on strike, protesting against supervision methods. Over the weekend that followed there was serious looting and rioting, and a monstrous crime wave. On the following Tuesday 500 specially enlisted volunteers restored order and the 638 strikers were sacked and never reinstated. So great was public outrage that there was no support for their re-employment. However, the cause of the problem was remedied.

The great Australian Aboriginal artist Albert Namatjira was such a successful ambassador for his people that he was granted full citizenship as an honorary white. This gave him access to liquor, which he was required by tribal law to share with family, relatives and friends. He was jailed for supplying alcohol to Aboriginal tribespeople. His death at the age of only 57 was probably hastened by the inability to cope with living between two cultures.

When the anti-Chinese riots of 1857 broke out in the Buckland River diggings of north-east Victoria many Chinese were killed and their tents burned. The troop of police which restored order was led by Robert O'Hara Burke, who subsequently died on his expedition to the north with William Wills. In fact it was the reputation Burke achieved in the suppression of the riot that led to his selection to lead the expedition.

Sport

The first English cricket team was brought to Australia by Messrs Spiers and Pond, a firm of Melbourne caterers. They brought them out as a second choice when the author Charles Dickens refused to make a lecture tour for them.

HOW BRAIN DAMAGE STARTS

Water-skiing was first displayed in Australia by Carl Atkinson who skied across Darwin Harbour in 1936. Later the same year he skied across Sydney Harbour but was cautioned by the water police not to commit the dangerous act again.

Rolf Harris, the Perth-born entertainer, was a swimming champion when young. At the age of 16 he was the junior Australian backstroke champion and the Western Australian senior backstroke champion from 1948 to 1952, when he left for London, fame and fortune.

Tony Roche, now a tennis coach of our junior hopefuls, nearly had his tennis career destroyed by a tennis elbow. However, a faith healer in the Philippines cured him completely and he went on to play top tennis for another 15 years.

The first person to develop hang-gliding kites was Bill Moyes from Sydney. In 1967 he was the first person to exceed a height of 300 metres (1000 feet) in a kite. He broke other records — by launching himself from snow skis on Mount Crackenback and flying about 4 kilometres (2½ miles) to Thredbo Village in 1968, and by setting an Australian endurance record of nearly seven hours. He also glided for eight minutes 32 seconds from the edge of the Grand Canyon in the U.S.A. In 1973 he set a new altitude record of 3260 metres (10,000 feet), and made a record glide of 22 kilometres (13 miles) when dropped from a hot air balloon.

Des Renford the Sydney-born marathon swimmer did not start marathon swimming until he was 40. He set many records including: first person to swim the English Channel 10 times; first person to swim the English Channel three times in one season; fastest crossing of Sydney Harbour; fastest time around Alcatraz; swimming the English Channel both ways with only a short break; swimming 40 laps of Bondi Beach (40 kilometres), then 50 laps (48

kilometres) the following year and swimming from Sydney to Wollongong (90 kilometres) in just over 27 hours. In June 1972 he broke the record for swimming across Sydney Harbour, then swam back again. He was the first person to complete the swim marathon course on the Derwent River (Tas.). He has won several match races and has competed all over the world.

The youngest Australian international sportsman so far was probably Ian Johnston who was cox of the Australian rowing crew at the Rome Olympics in 1960. He was only 13 years and three months.

The greatest axeman of all time was Jack O'Toole. Born at Warragul in 1917 he won his first world championship in 1947. In 1968, at the age of 52, he won both the world underhand and standing block championships. He competed in championships for 24 years and won 22 world championships. He was later president of the Axeman's Association. He died of a heart attack in 1983.

The winner of the Melbourne Cup in 1866 was The Barb. He won 15 races from 23 starts earning him the title of "The Black Demon". He won the Sydney Cup twice, in 1868 and 1869. His 1869 Sydney Cup win carrying 10 stone 8 pounds (66 kilograms) is the only time it has been won with such a weight.

When "The Barb" won the Melbourne Cup the judge was so excited by the finish between the winner and Exile that he forgot to place the third horse. The stewards met and decided that Falcon was third, but the bookmakers refused to pay out on the grounds that only the judge could make the decision. Their refusal was upheld by the authorities and the people who backed Falcon for the place lost their money.

The cry "Up there Cazaly" which was recently revived in a song, originated from the high marking skill of Roy Cazaly a South Melbourne star of the 1920s. When he flew for the ball his team-mate Harry Fleiter would shout "Up there Cazaly", and this was soon adopted by the crowd. It was even used as a battle cry by Australian troops in the second World War.

When Les Darcy, the boxer, died in America in 1917, his body was packed in ice and returned to Australia for burial. It was estimated that a crowd of one million people queued up to view his body as it lay in an open coffin in Sydney.

Australian crawl—this swimming stroke, the basis of all modern freestyle swimming, was originated by Alec Wickham, a young Solomon Islander working as a houseboy in Sydney. Until then the breaststroke and sidestroke were used by all swimmers.

Archer, winner of the first two Melbourne Cups in 1861 and 1862, was walked from Sydney to Melbourne, then home again—1000 kilometres (600 miles) each way—after winning, because he did not like the motion of boat travel.

Australian Rules football originated in 1858 with the Melbourne Football Club, which was formed to keep cricketers fit in winter. In Melbourne it has the greatest following per head of population of any field sport in the world.

The 1870 Melbourne Cup was won by Nimblefoot owned by Walter Craig of Craig's Hotel in Ballarat (Vic.). Walter Craig had a dream some months before the Cup where he saw the horse in his colours win the Cup—but the jockey

SPORT

was wearing a black armband. Mr Craig took this to mean that the horse would win but he would not live to see it. He told his friends of the dream and died on the following night.

In his first test match Don Bradman, who was 20 years of age, played against England making 18 and 1. He was dropped to 12th man in the next test. However in his career he scored 117 first-class centuries and, despite the comparatively small number of matches played, still figures prominently in the record books, over 30 years after retiring. Later created Sir Donald, Bradman was Australia's first cricketing knight.

Australian Edwin Flack won the 800 metres and 1500 metres running events at the first modern Olympics in 1896. He was an accountancy student in London and took time off to compete for Australia. In those days there was no official team. If you thought that you were good enough you just turned up.

Contrary to most reports there is nothing new about people yelling insults at cricketers. In 1895, Nat Gould in his book *On and Off the Turf in Australia* referred to spectators yelling insults at George Giffen who was the greatest cricketer of the period.

John Landy from Geelong (Vic.) was the first Australian to break four minutes for the mile. In Finland in 1954 he ran three minutes 58 seconds to break Roger Bannister's world record. He was only the second runner ever to beat the four minute barrier, which had been regarded as an impossible feat only a few years earlier.

One of Australia's great sporting identities was William Francis King, "the Flying Pieman". In 1848 he raced on foot against a coach and four horses from Windsor to Sydney and beat it by several minutes. Later the same month he bet that he could walk 192 miles (307 kilometres) in 48 hours; he won that one, too. For another bet he carried an 80 pound (36 kilogram) live goat over 1½ miles (2.5 kilometres) in 12 minutes. He also successfully raced a coach from Brisbane to Ipswich, but he had to carry a 20 pound (9 kilogram) pole as a handicap.

A night football match was played in Melbourne in 1879 under electric light. A reporter who covered the match said that "it was quite a spectacle, but spoilt by the players going out of sight in the dark patches".

In the early days of settlement, ploughing contests were a popular sport. Horse teams and bullocks were used and a half-acre (0.2 hectares) had to be ploughed in furrows 5 inches (13 centimetres) deep and 9 inches (23 centimetres) wide. Points were given for speed and accuracy. The interstate competitions came to an end in 1882 when the Victorians won all but one of the prizes.

Stanley Rowley won Australia's first Olympic medals for sprint running. At the Paris Olympics of 1900 he won a bronze medal in all three sprint events, the 60 metres, 100 metres and 200 metres.

Australia's first golf course was set out on the present site of the Flagstaff Gardens in Melbourne. It was set up in 1847 by a party of men from Scotland who formed Australia's first golf club. However, it closed in 1850.

The interstate cricket competition in Australia is for the Sheffield Shield. Lord Sheffield led the English team on

a tour of Australia in 1891-1892. He gave 150 guineas to be used in the promotion of Australian cricket, to buy a shield for the interstate competition, which was named after him.

The greatest victory by a Sheffield Shield team was by Victoria over New South Wales at Melbourne in 1926. Victoria made 1107 runs and won by an innings and 656 runs.

The world record for attendance at one day of a cricket match is almost 91,000. The crowd attended the Melbourne Cricket Ground in February 1961 for the second day's play in the final test of the series between Australia and the West Indies. There are many test matches in England where the total attendance is less than this.

Australia has far more registered players of lawn bowls than any other country in the world. Almost half of the world total belong to Australian clubs.

During her career in swimming Dawn Fraser broke world records 27 times.

"Snowy" Baker (1884-1953) has been described as the greatest all-round sportsman. He was a champion in 19 different sports. He was all-school athletics champion, played Rugby for Australia and rowed in a championship rowing eight. He played polo for Australia and won championships in diving, swimming, fencing, show-jumping, tentpegging, tilting, steeple-chasing and dressage. He won the Australian amateur middleweight boxing championship and a silver medal in boxing at the 1908 Olympic Games. He won over 20 wrestling contests. He played first-grade cricket and was a champion surfer winning several iron-man events. Later in life he acted in several movies in America.

Until the commencement of the modern Olympic Games in 1896 amateur running was practically nonexistent in Australia. Professional foot-running was important from the early 1800s. It was a major form of entertainment and gambling. Once amateur running grew, professional running declined.

Woodchopping is a sport completely dominated by Australians. Axe manufacturers in Australia have developed a specialised racing axe which is in great demand all over the world and the M-tooth cross-cut saw, which is the world's fastest saw.

Arguably the greatest billiards player of all time was Walter Lindrum (1898-1960). He was world billiards champion from 1932 to 1950, when he retired unbeaten. At one stage he was playing the next best players in the world, giving them 7000 points start. He raised vast amounts of money for charity.

Stuart Mackenzie the Australian rowing champion won the Diamond Sculls, the unofficial world championship of solo rowing, at Henley, England, for six years in a row from 1957 to 1962 inclusive.

The biggest sporting crowd ever, in Australia, was the crowd at the 1970 Australian Rules Grand Final in Melbourne. The crowd numbered 121,696 — about one per cent of the Australian population at the time.

The longest jump by a horse in Australia was by Solid Gold, which in 1936 at the Wagga Wagga Show (N.S.W.) jumped 36 feet 3 inches (11.05 metres) across water. The highest jump was by Gold Meade which jumped a fence 8 foot 6 inches (2.59 metres) high in Cairns in 1946.

SPORT

America, the yacht after which the America's Cup was named, finished its life in Australia. All that is known is that it was sold to a "private gentleman in Australia" in 1860.

Bill Northam (now Sir William), who won a gold medal for Australia at the 1964 Tokyo Olympics, was the oldest person to win an Olympic gold medal. He was 59 years of age and won it in the 5.5 metre class yachting.

Surfing made a late start in Australia because until 1903 it was against the law to bathe in the sea during daylight hours.

The great left-handed golfer Harry Williams won dozens of amateur tournaments but resisted turning professional. He lived with his widowed mother in Kew (Vic.). In 1961 he was unemployed and in financial trouble when he and his mother both committed suicide.

On the first tour by an English cricket team their star player George Griffiths played against a Beechworth XI by himself. He dismissed the Beechworth team for one run (which was a bye), then easily made the two runs for victory.

When E. H. Flack won the 800 metres run and 1500 metres run at the first modern Olympic Games in Athens in 1896 the officials did not have an Australian flag of any kind (not even a colonial flag for one the colonies.). So in confusion they raised the Austrian flag.

Melbourne's "Head of the River" boat races between the public schools once attracted crowds of nearly 100,000 people. When it could not be held on the Yarra River in 1947 because of construction work on the Swan Street Bridge it was shifted to the Barwon in Geelong. It has been held there ever since except for a disastrous experimental return to the Yarra in 1957, when widespread brawling and drunkenness spoiled the spectacle.

Although golf is popular in Australia it is played by only one person in every 35 of the population. In the United States it is played by about one person in 20, and in Canada by one person in every 12. Even in Japan it is played by one person in every 25.

In 1918 Solomon Islander Alick Wickham made a dive of 205 feet 9 inches (62.7 metres) into the Yarra River, Melbourne. A crowd of 60,000 people watched the feat. However it was claimed by Sir Frank Beaurepaire in 1956 that the height was really only 96 feet 5 inches (29.38 metres).

The lowest score made by a first-class cricket team in Australia was made by Victoria in 1904. They were all out for 14 against the M.C.C. (England).

Australia has a higher proportion of golf courses to its population than any other country, including the United States which ranks second. However in the United States an average of 950 golfers play at each course while in Australia the average is only about 400 per course.

The first century scored in test cricket was scored by Australian Charles Bannerman at Melbourne in 1877. He also scored the first century for Australia on English soil, in 1878. Ill-health forced him to give up cricket after only those two matches.

Ron Clarke the great Australian distance runner held world records for

2 miles, 3 miles, 5000 metres, 6 miles, 10,000 metres, 10 miles and 1 hour. However, he never won an Olympic gold medal. His best Olympic result was at Tokyo in 1964 when he won a bronze medal in the 10,000 metres.

The test match in which the Ashes originated, in 1882, was notable for the number of sevens involved. England scored 77 in the second innings, demon bowler Spofforth (Australia) took 7 wickets in each innings, Garrett and Boyle (Australia) bowled 7 maidens each in the first innings, Garrett bowled 7 overs in the second innings. Blackham (Australia) scored 17 runs in the first innings and 7 in the second. Steel (England) bowled 7 overs in the second innings. Not surprisingly, Australia won by . . . that's right, 7 runs.

Most sporting experts regard Herb Elliott as Australia's greatest-ever athlete. In his entire athletic career Herb Elliott was never beaten over 1500 metres or a mile. At one stage in his career he ran eight sub-four-minute miles in seven months. He won the gold medal for 1500 metres at the 1960 Olympic Games and many Commonwealth Games medals. He's still running, but now confines himself to around the streets of Hawthorn and Camberwell in Melbourne.

YOUNGEST AUSTRALIAN WINNERS

AUSTRALIAN RULES

Youngest Brownlow Medal Winner • Dinny Ryan (Fitzroy) in 1936, aged 19.
Youngest Sandover Medal Winner • John Todd (South Fremantle) in 1955, aged 16 years, 10 months in his first senior season.

BOXING

Youngest Australian Champion • Jackie Green (born Wellington, N.S.W., 12 November 1901) was 15 years, four months when he outpointed Al White to win the Australian flyweight title at Sydney (his title win was not recognised in Victoria).

CANOEING

Youngest Olympian • Sue Whitebrook was only 16 when she represented in the kayak pairs at Montreal in 1976. With Helen Jacopsohn she went close to reaching the finals, finishing fourth in a repechage race.

DIVING

Youngest Open Championships • Don Wagstaff and Janine Pelham were both 16 when they won National Open Championships in 1966 and 1974 respectively. Miss Pelham became the first Tasmanian to win a National Open Championship.

HORSE RACING

Melbourne Cup • Youngest jockey to win was Peter St Albans, who was only 13 when he won the 1876 Cup on Briseis. Racing historians are still unsure whether "St Albans" was the rider's real name. The horse was entered by the St Alban's stables and the coincidence appears to be too strong.

TROTTING AND PACING

Youngest Driver to Win the Interdominion • Chris Lewis was 20 when he won with Carclew at Adelaide in 1976.

SPORT

Golf

Youngest Winner of a Major Australian Championship • Harry Llewellyn Williams (1915–1961) was 16 when he won the Amateur Championship at The Australian, N.S.W. in 1931.

Hole-in-one Record Holder • Justin Gibson set a world record at the age of six years and 22 days, when he aced the 64 metre sixth hole at Albert Park, Melbourne, on 21 January 1979.

Billiards

Schoolboy champion, George Gray of Melbourne was at one stage ranked number 3 player in Australia while still at senior high school. Gray, like Fred Lindrum, made successful tours of Great Britain and on his 1910-11 tour, made 23 breaks of 1000 with a best of 2196. One of his world records (836 including 831 off the red) set in 1909 stood until the late 1920s. Gray made the break in a match against Fred Lindrum in Melbourne on 25 August 1909.

Skiing

Youngest International • Steven Clifford of N.S.W. was 15 when he represented Australia at the 1970 World Championships at Val Gardena, Italy. David Studley was younger than Clifford when he competed in America, but competed as an individual and not as an official Australian representative.

Squash

World Junior Championships • Australia entered this event for the first time in 1978 and the team of Greg Pollard, Kevin French, Ricky Hill and Tony Cameron and Glen Brumby emerged victorious in the finals in Sweden. Brumby won the World Junior Championship in 1978 and 1979.

Tennis

Youngest Champions
Australian Men's Singles • Ken Rosewall was 18 when he won in 1953.
Wimbledon Singles • Lew Hoad was 22 when he won in 1956.
Australian Women's Singles • Margaret Smith/Court was 18 when she won in 1960.
Wimbledon Singles • Evonne Goolagong/Cawley was 20 when she won in 1971.

Swimming

Shane Gould • (born Sydney, 1957) set a new world 100 metres record of 58.5 seconds in 1972 at the age of 15. In that single year she set new world marks for every recognised freestyle distance, won every Australian freestyle championship and won three gold medals at the Munich Olympics.

SKATEBOARD RIDING

The sport of skateboard riding was introduced to Australia in 1964 by a group of local surfers who had seen competitions in the United States. Former world champion surfer Bernard "Midget" Farrelly was among the pioneers. Lack of organisation resulted in the "boom" quickly coming to an end and the fad did not return until the early 1970s when new American skateboards, complete with advanced urethane wheels and other technical improvements, arrived in Australia. The Australian Skateboard Association was formed in 1975 and approaches to local councils to either build or lease suitable skating areas met with great success.

Early competitions were almost exclusively for downhill racing, but the dangerous nature of such events resulted in a strong swing to what is now known as "free form" competition in which skateboarders participate in events similar to surfing. Riders manoeuvre their boards in confined areas, usually constructed of smooth concrete, and earn points for performing difficult tricks in timed routines. The competition areas are invariably steeply banked and often include ramps (for jumping) and half pipes (for special trick riding).

The A.S.A. staged the first official Australian championships at Albany, Western Australia, in 1978 and included sections for seniors, juniors and girls. The venue, Albany Park, was the first "professional" skateboard centre constructed in Australia.

Since skateboard riding became properly organised in 1975, a number of professional troupes (many of them including champion surfers such as Cheyne Horan) have been formed for national exhibition tours. Other troupes were formed to give national safety demonstration exhibitions to overcome the poor early image of skateboarding caused by youngsters hogging footpaths and illegally riding on public roads. The first of these troupes was organised by the Broadmeadows City Council, Victoria, in 1975. It has been estimated that almost 200,000 Australians—mainly male aged 6–25—regularly participate in organised skateboard competitions. A movie, *The Ultimate Flex Machine*, aimed at youngsters in the 10–15 years group, was produced in the late 1970s.

AUSTRALIAN LITTLE ATHLETICS UNION

The Australian Little Athletics Union ranks as one of the most successful but least publicised enterprises in the history of sport in Australia. Established in 1964 to encourage girls and boys aged 5–15 years to take an interest in athletics, the Union now has almost 80,000 registered members. The main aim of the Union is to encourage participation rather than over-serious competition. The Union is comprised of associations in all States and all associations have affiliation with registered city and country athletic clubs. It is believed that on a per capita basis, the Little Athletics movement in Australia is the most successful in the world. The first Australian championships were staged in 1972 and since that time have been held in all States on a rotational basis. Competition events are staged under the same rules and conditions which exist at senior level, but those events which are considered too strenuous or potentially dangerous (pole vaulting, distance running, etc.) are excluded.

BMX

BMX (bicycle motocross), a pedal-powered version of motorcycle motocross, originated in California U.S.A. early in 1970. Riding ultra-lightweight, specially-designed bicycles, BMX competitors race on short dirt tracks (average length 400 m), modelled on motorcycle motocross circuits complete with hills, jumps, corrugated sections and banked turns.

The sport spread to Australia in the mid-1970s and the first track was built in 1977 on an old golf practice range on Epping Road, opposite the Channel Ten television studios. As BMX racing spread throughout Sydney and to other Australian cities, the Australian BMX Association was established to sanction clubs and organise competition meetings under rules laid down by the International BMX Federation.

The first official Australian championships were held in Sydney in 1981 and Jamie Hales (N.S.W.) won the inaugural Open Championship. Australia was first represented at the World Championships in 1983 when a team of 25 riders travelled to Saigren in Holland. Twenty-four Australians reached the finals and among the 17 who filled placings four won age championships. When only a token United States entry was received for the 1984 World Championships at Suzuki in Japan, Australian riders completely dominated the racing and won 14 titles.

The World Championships are open only to amateur riders, but BMX racing also caters for professionals. Amateur riders are able to compete against the professionals in Open meetings and, under international rules, can retain a small percentage of any prize money won provided it is used to cover travel costs to Australian and overseas meetings. The balance is held in trust by the Australian BMX Association.

In 1983 the Association revealed that there were 25,000 registered riders in Australia and this figure is likely to reach 27,000 during 1985. Boys in the 10-11 years age group dominate the ranks of competitors, but the sport is so popular that races are staged for riders as young as 8 years and, in recent times, for those over 40.

Racing in Australia falls into three competition brackets—for BMX machines (20 inch wheels), Cruisers (26 inch wheels) and Sidehacks (three-wheeled sidecars for rider and also a passenger who both balances the machine on corners and when necessary, pushes).

It is now possible to invest upwards of $1200 on a BMX machine and all necessary equipment—helmet, riding suit, special pads, gloves, boots and spares.

Australia has recorded a number of notable "firsts" in the sport, including the staging in September 1983 of the world's richest Pro-Am meeting at Sydney's Hordern Pavilion. The meeting, sponsored by Moove and Twisties, carried total prize money of $10,000. Following his win at the 1984 World Championships in Japan, Cameron Mitchell (then aged nine) of Woomelang, Victoria, became the youngest sportsman ever to be nominated for the prestigious ABC Sports Award and it is believed he is the youngest sportsperson in the world to be so honoured.

Among the many great BMX champions produced in Australia are: Dean Crisp of Jindalee, Brisbane, who set a record of 26 consecutive wins in 1984-85 and won the 1985 Australian Professional Championship: Leigh Egan, 17, of Victoria, a former top athlete who has won the World and Australian Open titles; Andrew

Figliomeni of Western Australia who has won World Championships for 3 successive years, 1983–85 and who also rides motorcycles in motocross competition; and girls Pauline Williams and Jackie Hawke, both of whom have won World Championships.

Australia now has a flourishing manufacturing industry producing BMX bicycles and associated equipment, and led the world by producing the first movie based on the sport, *BMX Bandits*. The "bible" of the sport in Australia is the colourful monthly newspaper, *Australasian BMX News*, first published in September 1983.

Australian BMX Champions

Australian World Champions

1983 Saigren, Holland
Andrew Figliomeni • 10 Years Expert
Andrew Figliomeni • 10 Years Open
Cameron Mitchell • Seven Years Expert
Cameron Mitchell • Seven Years Open
Lyndall Ellement • Seven Years and under Girls
Tracey Kosikowski • 12–13 Years Girls

1984 Suzuki, Japan
Leigh Egan • 14 Years and over Expert Open/17 Years Expert
Paul Addams • 16 Years Expert
John Duncan • 25 Years and over Cruiser
Trevor Sheppard • 18–24 Years and over Cruiser
Colin Wilson • 16–17 Years Cruiser
Andrew Figliomeni • 12 Years Expert
Brenton Cooper • 11 Years Expert
Cameron Mitchell • Eight to Nine Years Expert Open/Nine Years Expert
Darren Johnson • 10–11 Years Open
Pauline Williams • 16 Years Girls
Alana Madam • 12–13 Years Girls
Pamela Batista • Eight to nine Years Girls

1985 Whistler, British Columbia
Andrew Figliomeni • 13 Years Cruiser
Jackie Hawke • 16 Years Ladies Open

Australian Championships

1985 Launceston, Tasmania
Dean Crisp • No. 1 Plate Super Class
Leigh Egan • Open Class Champion
Pauline Williams • Ladies Open

Transport

When a bullock cart was bogged in the mud the bullocks did not always keep trying to pull it out. The less scrupulous bullocky would light a fire under their bellies to give them an incentive to pull out of the bog.

The first train to operate in Australia was a steam train that operated between Flinders Street, Melbourne, and Sandridge (now Port Melbourne). It was constructed by a private company to carry people from the port on their way to the goldfields. The first engine used was locally built but was a complete failure.

In the 1860s Cobb & Co introduced a "Leviathan" coach service between Ballarat and Geelong, which could carry over 90 passengers in less than comfort. It was drawn by 22 horses with three drivers and two outriders on the leading horses.

One well-known explorer did part of his work by bicycle. Donald Mackay (1870–1958) rode right around the Australian continent in 1899 and 1900, taking 243 days and mapping many features for the first time.

The biggest ship ever built in Australia was the ore carrier *Clutha Capricorn* of 83,000 tons (which is bigger than the *Queen Mary*). It was built at the Whyalla shipyard in South Australia.

The *Southern Cross*, first plane to cross the Pacific Ocean, is on permanent exhibition at Brisbane airport. In 1982 it was the subject of a bomb threat.

When camels were used for transporting goods in the outback, it was considered that a strong male camel could carry about 270 kilograms (600 pounds). Since a bale of wool weighed about 115 to 135 kilograms (250 to 300 pounds), one could be hung either side of the camel. When camels were used to haul railway sleepers for the Trans-Australia Railway they carried up to six sleepers on each side.

Before the second World War there were hundreds of kilometres of narrow-gauge railway lines used for hauling logs and other products throughout country Victoria. Very few of them

remain today, but some of the immense wooden trestle bridges still stand. Near Noojee (Vic.) are the remains of two wooden trestle bridges which were the biggest in the world in their day.

The first flight in a powered aircraft in Australia was made by F. Custance at Bolivar (S.A.) on 27 March 1910. The flight was made in a French-made Blériot monoplane.

The longest railway tunnel in Australia is the Woy Woy tunnel on the Sydney–Newcastle line. It is 1189 metres (3900 feet) long. This is very short by world standards.

Bullock drays always had trouble negotiating steep downhill sections. In order to help, the bullocky would often cut down a tree and attach it to the back of the dray to slow them up. Sometimes ropes were passed around trees and slowly let out, but if the rope broke the bullocks could have their necks broken by the sudden lurch forward.

The novice camel rider usually had trouble with parking. Old hands would await the critical moment when the camel knelt. In most cases when the camel dropped to its front knees the unwary rider would be pitched onto his or her face in front of the camel, to the delight of the spectators.

When camels were used in teams they were often used in single file — sometimes 20 and 30 in a row. This was to stop them kicking and savaging each other.

The first Cobb & Co. coaching route was the same as the first railway route several years later. It was from Melbourne to Sandridge (Port Melbourne). In 1854 regular services were provided to Bendigo, Ballarat and Castlemaine, and when rail services opened to these centres the headquarters was shifted to Bathurst in New South Wales to service the areas beyond the reach of railway lines.

Airlines which operate regularly in and out of Australia are Qantas, Air India, Air New Zealand, Air Nauru, Air Niugini, Alitalia, British Airways, Air Vanuatu, Air Pacific, Cathay Pacific, Canadian Pacific, Continental Airlines, Garuda, Japan Air Lines, J.A.T., K.L.M., Lufthansa, Malaysian Airline System, Singapore Airlines, United Airways, Philippine AirLines, South African Airways, Thai International and U.T.A.

The Qantas passenger fleet consists of 18 Boeing 747Bs, three Boeing 747 Combi convertible passenger/cargo aircraft; and one Boeing 747SP. Qantas currently operates nothing but jumbo jets and have six Boeing 767s on order.

The two major domestic airlines T.A.A. and Ansett carry approximately the same number of passengers each year, but T.A.A. has a slight edge in most years.

Australia's busiest airport is Kingsford Smith Airport at Mascot in Sydney which handles about 20 per cent more passengers than Tullamarine in Melbourne. Brisbane is next in importance; Melbourne's Tullamarine operates well under capacity.

The Australian national airline Qantas is the safest airline to travel with in the world, no matter which measure of safety is used. However, this is seldom publicised because it is thought that it may be unlucky, and also may put people off air travel by reminding them of the dangers.

TRANSPORT

New technology has often run into trouble with those displaced by it. The Afghan camel drivers had intense opposition from the drivers of horse, donkey and bullock teams who could not compete with their cheaper rates or the ability of the camels to travel overland away from the tracks. All sorts of methods were used to discourage them, from government Acts, to poisoning their camels.

Commercial flights to and from Australia did not begin until 1934, when Imperial Airlines and Qantas began a joint service between London and Brisbane.

The first inter-capital airline service in Australia started in 1924 when Australian Aerial Services began regular flights between Adelaide and Sydney.

Sydney's first powered trams were steam trams. There were so many complaints about their danger and dirtiness that Melbourne opted for cable-trams which were cleaner and safer but very slow. It took half an hour from Flinders Street to Richmond—about 3 kilometres (2 miles).

In March 1851 Dr William Bland, a Sydney surgeon, inventor and author, produced plans for a steam-driven dirigible which he claimed would make the Sydney–England trip in four or five days. He described this as his "atmotic ship". This preceded Zeppelin's airships by 50 years and was almost exactly the same craft. His plans were exhibited all over the world and were rejected by Emperor Napoleon III of France, Queen Victoria and President Abraham Lincoln. The plan lapsed due to lack of a substantial financial backer. Bland was later to become a member of parliament.

In the early days of the first settlement, bullocks were scarcer than human beasts of burden. Convicts were used to haul drays of produce to Sydney and to transport it around the town.

Bullocks were regarded as being greatly superior to horses as draught animals because they cost less to feed, were stronger, and cost about a quarter of the price. If they had an accident they could be slaughtered and salted for food and, when they were too old for the work could be fattened and sold to the butcher.

The early explorers found that a camel could go for a week without water, covering nearly 500 kilometres (over 300 miles). When water was available they might drink 54 litres (12 gallons) at a time.

On the regular routes coach horses were changed every 16 to 20 kilometres (10 to 12 miles), at the coaching stations. Crews were changed much less frequently.

Early timetables show that it took the Cobb & Co coach 16½ hours to travel the 170 kilometres (108 miles) from Colac to Hamilton in Victoria. The coach would leave Colac at 10 p.m. and reach Hamilton at 2.30 p.m. the following afternoon. Nowadays, by car it takes just over two hours.

The four founders of the coaching firm Cobb & Co. in 1853 were Freeman Cobb, John Peck, John Lamber and James Swanston. They were all Americans and made a fortune when the gold rush began.

River steamers penetrated the Murray River system as far as Albury (N.S.W.) on the Murray, Gundagai (N.S.W.) on the Murrumbidgee and Walgett

(N.S.W.) on the Darling near the Queensland border. Altogether over 6400 kilometres (4000 miles) of river were serviced by steamers.

In the 1870s there were more than 100 paddle steamers carrying passengers and cargo on the Murray River system, with Echuca (Vic.) being a major port. The coming of the railways, which were faster and more reliable, destroyed the industry by the 1920s.

The last Cobb & Co. coach route closed in 1924. It was the remote route from Surat to Yuleba near Roma in Queensland.

If there was no coach boy to open the gates on a coaching route the job fell to Chinese, Aborigines or young fit male passengers, in that order.

Not one Cobb & Co. driver was ever killed by bushrangers but several died in accidents, mainly due to downhill runaways.

Until the standard gauge line opened in 1962, passengers travelling between Sydney and Melbourne had to change trains at Albury. The two trains were parked either end of the same platform and passengers would walk from one to the other. Consequently it is claimed that Albury has the longest station platform in the world. It was probably just that it seemed that way.

The first electric railway in Australia opened on 20 May 1919 and was officially opened eight days later. It was from Essendon to Sandringham in Melbourne's suburbs.

Great problems were caused by the choice in each colony of differing rail gauges. In New South Wales they chose the British 4 feet 8½ inches (about 1.46 metres) which is now used by the Commonwealth Railways on the standard gauge line. In Victoria and South Australia 5 feet 3 inches (about 1.6 metres) was used. In the other States it was 3 feet 6 inches (about 1 metre). The mess this created was not intentional but was a result of poor coordination and lack of foresight. In the earliest days when the gauge decision had to be made, railways were short, novelty means of travel. It was never envisaged that they would actually link cities hundreds of kilometres apart.

In South Australia the first railway opened in 1854. It was the Port Elliot to Goolwa horse-drawn tramway, which took passengers and freight to and from the river boats on the Murray.

In the 1860s the quickest way to get from Adelaide to Sydney was by coach from Adelaide to Goolwa, by steamer to Echuca (Vic.) then by coach from Echuca to Sydney. Even by this quick route it took nearly a week. These days aircraft make the trip in under two hours.

Getting wool to market in the 1860s was quite a task. The wool from south-eastern South Australia would be hand-loaded onto bullock drays and battled cross-country to the river. There it would be unloaded by hand on the bank, and then lifted onto the steamer which took it to Goolwa. At Goolwa it was unloaded from the steamer and loaded onto drays pulled by horses, which were unloaded in Adelaide or at Victor Harbour.

The first Holden was the FX model which first came off the assembly line on 29 November 1948. The millionth Holden was sold in 1962. Holdens had market leadership in Australia from

1953 to 1982, when Ford just beat them. In many of those years there were more Holdens sold than all other passenger cars combined.

In 1937 Australia's 10 best-selling motor cars were, in order: Chevrolet, Ford Canadian, Vauxhall, Morris, Plymouth, Dodge, Austin, Oldsmobile, Pontiac, Buick. Most of these had locally built bodies put onto fully imported chassis and engines.

The first major Australian domestic airline was A.N.A.—Australian National Airways Pty Ltd—formed in 1936 by the combination of several small airlines. It dominated the domestic air transport industry until T.A.A. was set up in 1946. A.N.A. was taken over by Ansett Transport Industries in 1957, which called its airline Ansett-A.N.A. for several years before dropping the A.N.A. from its name. In that period Ansett also bought up several small airlines.

The hydrofoils from Circular Quay to Manly on Sydney Harbour take about 15 minute to make the journey compared with about 40 minutes on the ferry. The hydrofoils are imported from Italy.

The *Endeavour* barque in which Cook first explored Australia's east coast was much smaller than you may imagine. It was 32.3 metres (106.6 feet) long (that is about half as long against as a cricket pitch) and carried 12 guns and a crew of 71 men. It could sail in only 4 metres (13 feet) of water.

Our first fleet included 11 ships. There were two naval vessels, H.M.S. *Sirius* and H.M.S. *Supply*; six transports, the *Alexander, Charlotte, Friendship, Lady Penrhyn, Prince of Wales,* and *Scarborough*; and three storeships, the *Borrowdale, Fishburn* and *Golden Grove*. However, the whole fleet would have fitted quite comfortably inside a modern container ship.

The boat used by Bass and Flinders to explore the Botany Bay–George's River area was called *Tom Thumb*. It was only 8 feet long and 5 feet wide (2.5 metres by 1.5 metres).

Motor car ownership in Australia, taken as a proportion of population, is second only to the United States. In the United States there is a motor car for every two people, and in Australia for every 2.6 people. As a comparison, in the United Kingdom there is one for every four people and in Japan one for every six people.

The 180-year-old tradition of passenger shipping between England and Australia ended in the 1960s because ships could not compete with air transport. There are still 6000 or more freight ships visiting Australia every year and some do carry a few passengers. Recently, luxury cruises to Europe have commenced.

The first Australian roads followed the tracks of the explorers often from one blazed tree to another. The road often wound in and out of the large immovable trees and when it was sealed it still followed the same route. Parts of the Hume Highway near Holbrook (N.S.W.) were still like it until the last decade.

In the early days of the Port Arthur settlement in Van Diemen's Land (Tasmania) the convicts provided the motive power for transporting officials around the settlement. A railway was operated with carriages pushed by four running convicts. It was also used by the officials' wives and children for sightseeing trips.

Tucker

The macadamia nut or bopple nut is an Australian native species. However most of the world's commercial macadamia nuts are now grown in Hawaii. This was due to a reluctance by Australians to grow the tree commercially—however there are now commercial plantations in Queensland and New South Wales.

The fruit of the prickly pear can be eaten or used for jam. The cactus itself can be boiled if the prickles are removed. It is a gluey, bland vegetable but was a staple food of many Indian tribes in its native north America.

"Murrumbidgee jam" was a piece of bread soaked in cold black tea, then sprinkled with coarse brown sugar. A "Murrumbidgee oyster" was a raw egg with a pinch of salt and a sprinkle of vinegar eaten straight from the shell. But neither of these compared to the legendary "Murrumbidgee sandwich" which was a wild pig between two bags of flour or to the "Darling sandwich" which was a goanna between two sheets of bark.

Annual consumption of citrus fruits per head of population has increased since 1960 from 16 kilograms (35.2 pounds) per person to nearly 50 kilograms (110 pounds) per person. This is largely due to the growth of the fruit juice industry.

How would you feel about a Grabben Gullen pie—a small pumpkin scooped out in the centre, filled with chopped possum meat, then slowly baked. It is interesting that there was such an uproar about the sale of Tasmanian possum meat in Melbourne in 1983. In the early days it was regarded as a great delicacy and has been eaten by the Aborigines for over 30,000 years.

Australians have the world's highest per capita consumption of meat. This is probably traditional and also due to our relatively cheap prices. However, the consumption is dropping in every type of meat other than poultry. Australians consume over 100 kilograms (220 pounds) of meat per person per year. This compares with 15 kilograms (33 pounds) per year in Japan and 50 kilograms (110 pounds) in Britain.

Every year in Australia about 300 million chickens are killed for human consumption, which is about 20 for each person. In 1950, when they were comparatively more expensive, the figure was only three per person. Chicken is the fastest growing item of meat consumption in Australia.

Slices of corned beef fried in a batter of flour, milk and onions were known as "Burdekin ducks" or "Kimberley oysters".

Although the fruit of the Moreton Bay fig tree is edible and is eaten in large quantities by fruit bats, it has to be very ripe and purplish. Even then it does not compare well with cultivated figs.

More than 150,000 tonnes of bananas are produced in Australia in a year and virtually all of them are consumed in Australia. Despite the reference to Queenslanders as "bananalanders" a substantial part of the industry is centred around Coffs Harbour in New South Wales.

Small dampers or scones were known as johnny cakes, beggars-on-the-coals, devils-on-the-coals, and buck-jumpers. Probably because of their effect on the digestive system, they were also called death adders.

The old bush cooks often used Eno's Fruit Salts as a raising agent in their damper or cakes. Most of the time, though, it was too expensive for them to use.

Sodium alginate is a cream-coloured powder which forms a thick sticky solution used in wines, syrups, jellies, bread, thickened cream, icecream, adhesives and explosives. It is obtained from the giant kelp seaweed which grows off the eastern coast of Tasmania.

A particularly Australian food is the mutton bird. The greasy delicacy is captured on the islands of Bass Strait, including King Island. The fat fledglings of the short-tailed shearwater are captured from their burrows and smoked. They taste very oily and a little like bacon fat.

Although Australia produces over 20 million kilograms (44 million pounds) of honey a year, of which a large part is exported, none of it is from native bees. The Australian honey bee makes its hives in hollow trees and does not sting. However, its production is not of sufficient quantity or quality for it to be used commercially. Most of the commercial bees in Australia have been bred from Italian bees.

There is an old bush saying, which may not be a complete myth, that a man is not a good shearers' cook unless he can make a tasty soup out of a pair of old socks.

Gardeners have great trouble with a persistent weed called "fat hen". It has been used as a type of spinach for thousands of years and was the major green vegetable in Britain until the 19th century.

That delicious Australian invention, the pavlova, was named after the Russian ballerina Pavlova who visited Australia in 1926 and 1929. It was named for her lightness. The dish was concocted by chef Henry Sachse of the Esplanade Hotel in Perth in 1935. Overseas, only those educated and enlightened by Australians have heard of it.

Scallops are regarded as a delicacy. The part which is eaten is really the muscle that opens and closes the shells. The creature swims by a kind of jet propulsion where shells are opened and

closed in a clapping motion forcing water through the jets. The muscle which controls the shells and grows large from this activity is eaten; the remainder of the creature is not edible.

The great chef Escoffier used wattle flowers to make fritters. The flowers were steeped in brandy and sugar for three days. They were then mixed in a light pancake batter to make crisp fritters which were served with sugar and whipped cream.

An old bush favourite was "Gundaroo bullock", named after the town of Gundaroo in New South Wales. It was the bushmen's name for koala meat.

An old bush method for keeping meat fresh in the hot weather was to submerge it in sour milk or buttermilk, and rinse it well when it was to be used.

One of the best-known weeds in Australia is the dock. All forms of this weed may be used as green vegetables although some are quite bitter. Dandelions and stinging nettles are also used as spinach substitutes in parts of Europe and are quite nutritious. Stinging nettles are not recommended as a salad vegetable.

"Blackfellow's bread" is a type of fungus which grows just below the ground's surface and is often revealed by ploughing. There is no evidence that it was ever eaten by the Aborigines although it is edible.

The "Diamantina cocktail" was a Queensland drink from the Diamantina River area. It is difficult to know whether they really drank it or used it as a joke on new settlers. It consisted of a bottle of Bundaberg rum, a can of condensed milk and an emu egg.

Over half the milk produced in Australia is used for butter making. Only 24 litres (about 5.3 gallons) out of every 100 (about 22 gallons) are sold as fresh milk and 10 (about 2.2 gallons) are used for cheese. Despite the production of all that butter, margarine outsells it by more than two to one.

In Australia we use over 5000 million litres (1,100 million gallons) of milk every year and over 871,000 tonnes (857,000 tons) of potatoes, which is fair enough, but how about 350,000,000 litres (77,000,000 gallons) of wine — over 20 litres (4.4 gallons) per person.

There is an old bushman's recipe for boiled cockatoo. Select three average-size stones and place in a billy of water with the plucked cockatoo. Place over a hot fire and boil hard for 10 hours and simmer for another six. Tip out the water, give the cockatoo to the dog and eat the stones.

Early settlers from southern Europe were supposed to have made a delicious pie from "ha-ha pigeons", as they called them. One presumes that they were kookaburras.

The most important vegetable crops in Australia in terms of production are: potatoes 800,000 tonnes; tomatoes 200,000 tonnes; peas 140,000 tonnes; onions 110,000 tonnes; carrots 100,000 tonnes; cabbage and brussels sprouts 90,000 tonnes; cauliflowers 80,000 tonnes; green beans 45,000 tonnes; lettuce 38,000 tonnes. Victoria has the largest acreage under commercial vegetables.

The Peach Melba dessert was named after Dame Nellie Melba. In its original form it should be vanilla icecream with sliced peaches and Melba sauce (raspberry purée), but in most cases these days coloured flavouring is substituted for the Melba sauce and ground peanuts are added.

The great Australian delicacy "the floater" is not exactly aesthetically exciting. It is a hot meat pie floating in a plate of pea soup. Those with palates experienced in the floater's pleasures advise novices to refuse it if the pie sinks—the soup must be too thin.

Damper was a standard food in the outback. It was bread baked in the ashes of a camp fire or in a camp oven. It was usually a circular flat cake, about 5 or 6 centimetres (2 or 3 inches) thick and up to 0.5 metre (2 feet) across. It was cut into wedges like a cake and tasted like a crisp scone. Despite statements to the contrary in some books, it was not always unleavened—rising agents such as baking powder, cream of tartar and Eno's Fruit Salts were often used. The name damper arose from the water used to make the dough.

Some other terms used in the old days in the outback were:
flyswisher stew—oxtail
dust—flour
dynamite—baking powder
flybog—jam
bee jam—honey
leprosy—cabbage
goldfish—tinned herrings or sardines
ointment—custard

Vegetation

The pisonia, a small softwood tree which grows in Queensland and northern New South Wales, is sometimes called a bird-catching tree. Small birds cannot escape from the tree when their wings or feathers adhere to its sticky fruits.

The beautiful jacaranda tree with its delicate mauve flowers which flourishes in warm coastal regions of Australia is regarded by most people as a native tree. It is, however, native to Brazil and was introduced by commercial nurseries.

During the second World War there was a rumour that the yacca plants which grow in low-lying boggy areas were used to make explosives. In fact this is quite possible. The resin of this plant can be used in varnishes, stains, polishes and lacquers and is a source of picric acid which is an explosive.

The paperbarks (Melaleucas) are pleasant ornamental shrubs and trees that earn their name from their bark which peels off in strips. They are also the source of a valuable medicinal oil called oil of cajeput.

Wattle trees (Acacias) got their common name from their use in the building of "wattle and daub" houses. This method of building uses twigs (wattle) and mud (daub) to form walls which harden in the sun. The twigs of what is now called the "black wattle" were ideal for the purpose. The tree was named after the use, not the other way around.

The Norfolk Island pine is a conifer, native to Norfolk Island, which has been used widely throughout Australia, particularly near beaches and in coastal areas. Although it is a useful source of softwood timber, it is not a true pine tree.

The mulga is a small shrubby tree which grows in most inland areas. Its timber has pleasing contrasting colours of dark-brown and yellow and can be highly polished. It is used for carved curios and souvenirs. The Aborigines used it to make shields, prizing its hardness.

Mallee scrub is the vegetation cover in many semi-desert areas of southern

VEGETATION

Australia. It comprises a number of species of eucalypt with many stems growing from long rootstocks known as lignotubers. It is almost as if the trunk is underground and the branches are growing upwards from it. Many eucalypts have the ability to adapt in this way to harsh conditions. Most mallee species if transplanted to better areas develop as normal single-trunk trees. The mallee roots are used as firewood in open fireplaces because they burn for long periods, giving out great heat.

Mangrove swamps occur in many of Australia's coastal regions, but seldom on the south coast. In many species the mangrove roots travel horizontally for some distance and send up many air roots which project above the mud and help aerate the main root system. The seeds germinate while they are still on the tree and the roots often reach the mud before the fruits drop. Mangrove swamps, once regarded as useless and suitable only for reclamation, are now regarded as valuable habitats for the breeding of fish and birdlife.

The beautifully fragrant boronia, which is a favourite of Australian gardeners, has about 90 different species. They are part of the citrus group, closely related to lemons and oranges.

The manna gums are so-called because for part of the year a sweet white substance occurs on the leaves and buds. It was used by the Aborigines to make a sweet drink and sweeten foods.

Although the Aborigines used hundreds of native plant species for food, only one, the macadamia nut, has been used as a commercially produced food. There are dozens of species with potential simply awaiting enterprise and development.

Paterson's curse (or salvation Jane) which covers thousands of hectares of farmland in eastern Australia was spread from one garden specimen introduced by a farmer called Paterson, near Albury (N.S.W.). It can be eaten by stock only when the plant is very young; when mature it is poisonous.

Leptospermum species, or tea-trees, are sometimes incorrectly spelt "ti-trees". The name comes from Captain James Cook's journal which told of a pleasant concoction made from leaves of the tea plant. Trials with the leaves may convince you that you are not using the same plant that he was.

The Australian eucalypts are very well adapted to fire. The trunk and limbs have special nodes which are softened by fire, and new growth sprouts from these within a month of the fire. Other types of trees, such as deciduous trees and pines, are usually killed completely by fire.

In 1872 a mountain ash was cut down in Gippsland (Vic.) which measured 132.6 metres (435 feet) to the point where its trunk had snapped off. It is estimated that it would probably have been over 152 metres (500 feet) in its prime. There is a stand of mountain ash at Cambarville (Vic.) with trees over 91 metres (300 feet). These are the tallest trees left in Australia.

Scientists agree that because of the weight/strength relationship of timber it is not possible for trees to grow much taller than 90 metres (300 feet) without breaking in the wind. The stands of mountain ash *Eucalyptus regnans* in the Cumberland Valley (Vic.) which are around this height are severely wind damaged.

A macrozamia pine which grows in the

garden of the Hotel St Bernard in Tamborine (Qld) is reputed to be 10,000 years old. If this is true, it makes America's 5000-year-old bristlecone pines look young.

Roly-poly is the name given to several species of plants that break loose from the soil and roll across the land, building up against the fences. They are not related to the American tumbleweed which has become naturalised in some inland areas.

There are seven Australian species of sandalwood including the white sandalwood which is used in incense sticks and for its oil. Sandalwoods are semi-parasitic on the roots of other trees. Common trees related to the sandalwood are the quandong and the native cherry.

There are over 15,000 different varieties of wheat kept in the Australian Wheat Collection at Tamworth (N.S.W.) to supply genetic material for wheat growing. Only about 15 of these are widely grown.

The great baobab trees that grow in the Kimberley district of Western Australia are often hollow in the centre. In the old days they were used to temporarily hold prisoners. There is one at Derby (W.A.) called the "Prison Tree" which was used for this purpose for several years.

The kurrajong trees found in inland New South Wales, Victoria and southern Queensland are valuable not only as shade trees in the outback areas. They can be stripped of their foliage which is then used as fodder for sheep and cattle in times of drought.

The black wattle is cultivated in many overseas countries for its bark which is used for tanbark in the tanning process. In the early days of Victoria this was also a major industry in the Portland (Vic.) area, but the industry died out. These days our wattle trees are not used for this purpose at all.

Before they were destroyed by the cactoblastis grubs, the prickly pear plants in Queensland and northern New South Wales were a major problem. In the 1920s they covered over 200 million hectares (about 50 million acres) of farming land.

Australian red cedar is a beautiful timber used in cabinet making, but has now been largely cut out and is available only in small quantities. The best cedar came from the Richmond River Valley in northern New South Wales. Coffs Harbour developed largely as a port for the cedar trade.

Although eucalypts are called "gumtrees", this is a misnomer because they do not produce gum. Some of them, particularly the bloodwoods, exude a dark material called "kino" which is a resin containing tannin. It is thought that this was the material referred to by Captain Arthur Phillip when he first described them as "gumtrees".

Most of the pastures used for grazing in Australia consists of introduced species of grass. Very little in the way of native grass is used except in the northern and inland open growing areas. Native grasses are mostly coarse and grow in tufts, but many are suitable for grazing and are less prone to drought.

War

Did you know that Australia became involved in the American Civil War? In January 1865 the Confederate warship *Shenandoah* visited Port Phillip Bay and demanded the use of maintenance facilities. It threatened to bombard Melbourne with its guns if facilities were not provided, so they were granted. Afterwards the *Shenandoah* sailed into the Pacific and sank the Union's whaling fleet. As a result the British Government had to pay $U.S. 15 million compensation to the American Government.

In 1914 the German ship the *Pfalz* was moored at Melbourne's Victoria Dock on the eve of declaration of war with Germany. When war was declared the captain tried to leave Port Phillip Bay after being ordered not to do so. A shot was fired across the bows of the ship from a shore battery at Flinders. This was the first shot fired by the British Empire in the first World War. The pilot persuaded the captain to return to port and the ship was interned.

The first engagement by the newly formed Royal Australian Navy was the battle between the Australian cruiser HMAS *Sydney* and the German light-cruiser *Emden* off the Cocos Islands on 9 November 1914. The *Emden* ran aground and surrendered.

When Darwin was first attacked by the Japanese in 1942 the planes flew over Melville Island and the missionaries radioed Darwin giving 20 minutes warning. However, the Australian Airforce failed to take any action and the Darwin alarm was not sounded until they saw the bombs falling. Over 20 planes were destroyed on the ground.

Twenty-two Australian pilots fought in the British squadrons at the Battle of Britain in 1940. Of these 14 were killed, a death rate of 63 per cent.

There were over twice as many Australian soldiers killed in the fighting in the first World War as there were in the second World War. 59,342 were killed in the first World War and 29,400

in the second World War (although an additional 8000 died in Japanese prison camps).

Australia's defence plans during the second World War included the Brisbane Line. This was a plan for the Australian Army to withdraw to a base line drawn from Adelaide to Brisbane to defend south-eastern Australia only. It was heavily criticised in Queensland and Western Australia, but there was never any need for it to be tested.

Ninety-six Australians have won the Victoria Cross which is the Commonwealth's highest military decoration. It was not possible for members of colonial forces to win it until 1867, although the award itself dates from 1856.

About one in every eight Australian soldiers killed in the first World War (7818 out of 59,342) was killed at Gallipoli, one of the greatest military disasters of all time. If it is possible to blame anyone, the ultimate responsibility probably lies with Winston Churchill, who was first lord of the Admiralty and suggested the Gallipoli campaign.

When the hospital ship *Centaur* was torpedoed by a Japanese submarine in 1943, there were 268 people lost. Some people have since claimed that it was carrying ammunition and the outrage that arose from the incident was largely misplaced.

When Darwin was first bombed on 19 February 1942, damage was much greater than was admitted at the time. Over 250 people were killed (including 53 civilians) and nearly 400 were injured. Half of the people killed were in the six ships that were destroyed, but there was heavy damage, particularly to government offices. At the time people feared that it was a softening up for invasion, and stories are told of the panic evacuations to the south, but the Japanese were making a pre-emptive strike to prevent an attack on their division in the Netherlands East Indies (now Indonesia), and their plan was not to make a landing in Australia until much later, if at all.

Among the tragic sinkings of the second World War was the loss of the HMAS *Kuttabul*. This was a depot ship tied up in Sydney Harbour when the harbour was infiltrated by Japanese midget submarines in June 1942. It was sunk by a torpedo and 19 lives were lost among the naval ratings who were using it as a dormitory.

Coastwatchers under control of the Australian Navy were stationed on the islands north of Australia to report on enemy movements by air, sea and land. One such coastwatcher in the Solomon Islands reported the sinking of the U.S. Patrol Boat 109 on 1 August 1943, which led to the crew being rescued. The boat's commander was John F. Kennedy, later to become president of the U.S.A.

Australian prime minister for 1968–71, Sir John Gorton, was a fighter pilot. His rugged features are the result of facial injuries suffered when he was shot down in his R.A.A.F. Hurricane fighter at Singapore in 1942.

The R.A.A.F. operates 16 front-line squadrons based throughout Australia and at Butterworth in Malaysia. However only two squadrons of F-111s and three squadrons of Mirage 111 OAs are equipped for modern warfare. Aircraft like the "Canberra" jet bombers are still in operational use after about 30 years.

WAR

The Royal Australian Navy is smaller than that of any other country with a large coastline to defend. Since the scrapping of the aircraft carrier *Melbourne*, it consists of 5 small destroyers of 4500 tons, 9 frigates of about 3500 tons, 6 submarines, 3 small minesweepers and 12 patrol boats.

The worst naval disaster suffered by the Royal Australian Navy was the sinking of HMAS *Sydney* on 19 November 1941. She was sunk and all 645 men on board were killed by the German auxiliary cruiser *Kormoran*. It happened about 240 kilometres (150 miles) off the Western Australian coast.

In the Boer War more Australians died from disease than died from enemy action. Two hundred and fifty-one were killed in action, 267 died of disease and 882 were wounded.

The first Australian warship to be sunk in action in the second World War was HMAS *Waterhen*, sunk off the Libyan coast on 30 June 1941 by German aircraft. It was a destroyer of 1118 tons; there were no casualties.

During the second World War the U.S.A. supplied arms and material to Australia worth £1500 million, but Australia only paid $U.S.54 million of the debt because of an agreement made in 1945.

The first Australian warship to be sunk in the second World War was the HMAS *Goorangi*. This auxiliary minesweeper of 226 tons collided with the M. V. *Duntroon* in Port Phillip Bay on 20 November 1940 and all 24 people on board were killed.

At the most recent count there were 72,518 people in Australia's permanent forces and another 32,737 in the reserves. Of our permanent forces, 4326 were women.

In June 1942 about a week after the midget submarine attack on Sydney Harbour, the Sydney suburbs of Rose Bay and Bellevue Hill were shelled, probably by the mother ship. Little damage was done, but in the panic many house owners sold their properties cheaply because they feared an invasion.

In the second World War about 300,000 Australians left to fight, 60,000 died and 120,000 were seriously injured. No other part of the British Empire suffered anything near this casualty rate.

The first flagship of the Australian navy, the dreadnought *Australia*, was scuttled off Sydney Harbour as part of a reorganisation of Allied forces between the two World Wars.

The first Victoria Cross won by an Australian in the second World War was won by John Hurst Edmondson — on 13 April 1941 at Tobruk he engaged the enemy in hand-to-hand fighting although badly injured. He saved his officer's life and helped defeat the enemy attack, but he died from his injuries.

Darwin was first bombed on 19 February 1942. During the second World War it was bombed 64 times with the last attack on 12 November 1943. Nine other towns were bombed, including Broome (W.A.) and Townsville (Qld).

The first well-known Australian Rules footballer to be killed in the second World War was Ron Barassi (Snr), father of the famous Melbourne coach. The Barassis' Italian ancestors migrated to Australia in 1857.

The Australian colonial forces who made a big show of going to the Sudan War in 1885 arrived after all the fighting was over. They spent most of their time on railway fatigue, except for a small contingent who were detached to form part of a camel corps. Six of them died of fever before the force arrived back in Australia.

Australia sent a naval force to China to assist Britain in quelling the Boxer Rebellion in 1900. The China naval contingent consisted of New South Wales, Queensland and Victorian troops transported in H.M.A.S. *Wallaroo*, the liner *Salamis* and the South Australian gunboat H.M.S.A.S. *Protector*. However they did not actually fight in the uprising, but merely acted as a deterrent by sailing off the coast.

Due to wartime fears Queensland suspended compulsory school attendance from 1941 to October 1944.

On New Year's Day 1915 at the height of the first World War, in which Turkey fought on the German side, two Turkish icecream vendors from Broken Hill opened fire on a train of picnic-goers. Six people died in the "Battle of Broken Hill", including the two Turks, and many were wounded. As a result, all enemy nationals were interned for the remainder of the war.

For the first two years of the second World War the Menzies Government concentrated mainly on the defence of Britain. Australian troops were deployed all over Europe and North Africa, leaving Australia largely undefended until the Americans entered the war in 1941.

The first Australian-built warship was the *Spitfire*, a 65 ton wooden ketch carrying a 32-pounder gun astern on an adjustable carriage. This was the pride of the New South Wales Navy in 1855. Most of the New South Wales Navy consisted of the land-based Naval Brigade, equipped with horses to ride from point to point on the coast and repel invaders.

The Duntroon Military College in Canberra was set up on Lord Kitchener's recommendation on his visit to Australia in 1912. These days it is regarded as one of the premier military academies in the world.

In 1916, at the request of the British Government, the Australian Government proposed to introduce conscription for military service. A referendum was held and the "No" campaign was successful. The result:
No—1,160,033 people; New South Wales, Queensland and South Australia.
Yes—1,087,557 people; Victoria, Tasmania and Western Australia.
In a second ballot held in 1917 the "No" majority increased:
No—1,181,747 people; New South Wales, Queensland, South Australia and Victoria.
Yes—1,015,159 people: Tasmania and Western Australia.

Food rationing was introduced in Australia in the second World War in mid-1942. At its most severe, rationing provided for each person each week—2 ounces (60 grams) of tea, 1 pound (450 grams) sugar, 6 ounces (170 grams) of butter, and 2¼ pounds (1 kilogram) of meat. Sausages, poultry, offal, fish and bacon were not rationed. Clothing was also rationed.

At the height of the second World War, Winston Churchill decided that he wanted a platypus, no reasons given. It

was carefully transported by ship then transferred to a submarine for the last three days of the trip. The shock of a depth-charge attack on the submarine killed it. It is still not known why Churchill wanted it.

In 1943 six Australian commandoes were taken by a captured Japanese fishing boat to Singapore where they attached limpet mines to seven Japanese ships in the harbour. 40,000 tons of Japanese shipping was sunk and the men all returned safely to Exmouth Gulf three weeks later. However, later in the war all six of them were killed in action.

When the Japanese prisoners broke out of the prisoner of war camp at Cowra (N.S.W.) on 5 August 1944 the death toll was 234 Japanese and three Australian guards. The Japanese soldiers refused to surrender even against overwhelming odds.

The greatest Australian air ace was Captain R. A. Little who shot down 47 enemy aircraft in the first World War. He was killed in June 1918. In the second World War the best effort was by Group Captain Clive Caldwell with 28½ kills (the ½ indicating a shared kill).

When "Breaker" Morant and P. J. Handcock were executed during the Boer War the Australian public was not told until after it was over. Largely as a result of this, in later wars Australians controlled their own disciplinary action and it was a rule that volunteers could not be executed.

The first action by Australian troops in the second World War was at Bardia in Libya. The action to take the town, held by Italian troops, started on 3 January 1941. By 5 January the town was taken and the Australians had over 40,000 prisoners.

The R.A.A.F.'s flying school was founded at Point Cook (Vic.) in 1913. It was selected as a site because it was on the coast of Port Phillip Bay and was therefore suitable for seaplanes as well as land-based planes. However, seaplanes went out of fashion and were not used by the R.A.A.F.

During the second World War an extreme nationalist group called the "Australia First Movement" was formed. Its members believed that Australia should look after its own interests rather than let Australian troops be used in the overall Allied strategy. They were opposed to any use of Australian troops beyond New Guinea.

Major-General Sir W. T. Bridges, commander of the Australian forces at Gallipoli, was one of the casualties of the campaign. He was killed when a sniper's bullet severed a thigh artery.

Women

Most people know that the 1912 competition for designs for the city of Canberra was won by Walter Burley Griffin. What is not widely known is that it was won jointly with his fiancée, Marion Mahony.

Women were not admitted as students to Australian universities until 1881. At the time female entrance to tertiary education was regarded by many (not all of them men) to be an outrageous move.

The first woman to fly solo from England to Australia was Amy Johnson (1903-1941). She was drowned in 1941 when she baled out from a crashing aircraft over the Thames Estuary in England.

Caroline Chisholm (1808-1877) is regarded as a saint. After living in India with her army lieutenant husband, she came to Sydney in 1838. She spent her time assisting penniless and destitute migrant women. In 1866 she returned to England where she died in 1877, after years as an invalid.

While famous for her work in various social reforms, less well known is the fact that Caroline Chisholm's life had an influence on that of Florence Nightingale. The Nightingale family only allowed Florence to go nursing because "Mrs Chisholm had put some respectability into nursing" as a profession.

Linda McGill (born 1945) was the first Australian to swim the English Channel (7 August 1965). She broke the record for that swim on the third occasion she swam it. She has broken many swimming records since, including being the first person ever to swim across Port Phillip Bay at its widest point—40 kilometres (25 miles).

"Granny Smith" apples were first grown at North Ryde, now part of Sydney. Granny Smith emigrated with her family from England in 1839. They had a fruit orchard and Granny used to take her fruit to the Sydney market. She was given some green apples known as "Tasmanian French crabs" to try as cookers and threw the peels and cores out of the kitchen window. In time a

WOMEN

tree grew outside the window which was the first "Granny Smith". They are regarded as the best general utility apple, even today, nearly 150 years later. All present "Granny Smiths" have sprung from that first tree.

Anybody who knows any history has heard of John Macarthur, but his wife Elizabeth Macarthur has much less recognition despite the fact that even Macarthur himself regarded her as an equal partner. During her husband's exile in England and his business trips, it was Elizabeth who was responsible for breeding the quality flocks of sheep and improving the wool. Her husband appears on the $2 note for his contribution to the wool industry. Perhaps it should be Elizabeth who has that honour.

When the hospital ship *Centaur* was sunk off the Queensland coast in 1943 the heroine was Sister Eleanor Savage. She was the sole surviving nursing sister and she set up a floating first aid station on a large piece of wreckage. She also took charge of the small supply of food and rationed it out. After two days the survivors were rescued by an American destroyer.

Heather McKay (nee Blundell) must be close to being the greatest Australian sportswoman of all time. She won the world championship of women's squash 12 years in a row from 1962 to 1973. In that 12-year period she lost only one match. She also played hockey for Australia in 1967.

Decima Norman was Australia's first great woman athlete. She won a record five gold medals in Sydney, at the 1938 Empire Games. She won the 100 yards, 220 yards and the long jump, and was a member of the 440 yards and 660 yards relay teams. Except for the 660 yards relay, the times were Empire Games records. Only recently has her achievement received the recognition it deserves.

Grace Bussel was the 16-year-old daughter of a settler near the coast 250 kilometres (155 miles) south of Fremantle. In 1876, she was mustering stock when she saw the steamer *Georgette* aground and its passengers and crew fighting for their lives in the surf. For about four hours she and a native stockman rescued survivors and then she rode about 20 kilometres (12 miles) across country to fetch help. She was presented with a medal from the Royal Humane Society in 1878.

In 1881 Mary Watson was alone on Lizard Island off the North Queensland coast with two Chinese servants and a young baby. The Aborigines came and speared both Chinese, eating one of them. There was no boat, but Mrs Watson placed provisions, herself, the baby and the wounded servant in an old iron tank used for boiling bêche-de-mer and sailed it for the mainland. After two days they were grounded on a reef and made it to Watson Island. Unfortunately they all died of thirst but a journal kept by Mary Watson was found next to her body in the tank.

Emily Lacey was thrown into the water when the steamer *Quetta* struck a submerged rock in 1890. She swam in the direction of land and was almost unconscious when she was picked up by the steamer *Albatross*. She was wrecked at 8.30 on Friday night, and was taken from the water at 8.10 on Sunday morning. She had been in the water for almost 36 hours and survived.

Charlotte Badger started life as a pickpocket in London and was transported in 1806. She was assigned to

work on the colonial brig *Venus*. With her convict companions she seized the ship near Hobart and they set sail for New Zealand. In the Bay of Islands they destroyed the *Venus* and lived with the local Maoris. In 1818 Charlotte left New Zealand with the captain of a New Zealand whaler and nothing more was heard of "Australia's woman pirate".

There were no women's events at the Commonwealth (Empire) Games until 1934. At those 1934 games, Australia's only woman gold medallist was C. Dennis who won the 200 yards breast-stroke swim.

The first woman swimmer to break 60 seconds for a 100 metres swim was Dawn Fraser. She achieved this swimming for Australia at the Tokyo Olympics of 1964. She had already won the same event in 1956 and 1960.

Australia's first star of the silent movies was Lottie Lyall. Unfortunately she died of tuberculosis in 1925 when she was only 34 years of age.

The highest bravery award to be won by an Australian woman is the George Cross. Joan D. Pearson of Melbourne won it in 1940 for an aircraft rescue in Britain. The only higher award for bravery is the Victoria Cross which can only be won in war and Australian women (so far) have not been involved in front-line fighting.

Louisa Lawson, mother of the great Australian author Henry Lawson, invented a brass buckle for sealing mailbags. Eventually it was accepted for use by the postal authorities, but a manufacturer copied her idea and any profits she may have made were lost in the legal action that followed.

The first woman to be registered as a doctor in Australia was Dr Constance Stone, in Melbourne in 1890.

The first woman Labor member of any Australian parliament was Miss Mary Holman, elected to the Western Australian Parliament in 1925.

Mary Bryant was the first female transported convict to return from Australia to England. With a group of convicts and her children she stole Governor Phillip's cutter. They discovered coal at Newcastle, fought off the Aborigines several times and were arrested in Timor and taken to Batavia by Dutch officials. Mary Bryant was sent to England in 1792 and tried for escaping. The death sentence which was usually passed on escaped convicts was commuted and eventually, after public sympathy was aroused, she was pardoned and given a small pension, as were the other escapees. She died in England.

The great singer Gladys Moncrieff (1892-1976) was badly injured in a car accident in 1938 and could do only radio and light concert work until she completely recovered in 1942.

The first Australian woman ever to win a gold medal in the Olympics was Fanny Durack who won the 100 metres freestyle swim at the Stockholm Olympics of 1912. She established a world record of 79.8 seconds. The record is now under 60 seconds.

The first woman to be admitted to the Bar to practise as a barrister in Australia was Ada Emily Evans, admitted in Sydney in 1902. Even today there is resistance to women barristers and many of them practise only in family law. The first woman Q.C. in Australia was Roma Mitchell (now a Justice) who became a Q.C. in 1962.

WOMEN

In Charles Dickens's *Great Expectations* a major character is Miss Havisham who lives in a room of cobwebs that has remained untouched since she was jilted on her wedding day. Miss Havisham was based on the true story of Eliza Donnithorne who lived at Newtown in Sydney in a house called "Cambridge Hall". She lived as a recluse after having been jilted, and the room containing the wedding breakfast was left untouched until after her death 40 years later in 1888. Miss Donnithorne never left the house in the whole of that 40 years.

Queen Elizabeth is the longest-ruling monarch of Australia. The title dates from the Statute of Westminster in 1931 and she is the fourth ruler we have had in that period of time.

Mary Reibey, who is often described as Australia's first businesswoman, came to Australia as a convict. One of her grandchildren became premier of Tasmania, another was a knighted judge.

Australia's first female politician was Edith Cowan, who was elected to the Western Australian Parliament in 1921. She was a Nationalist Party member.

Australia's first woman senator was Mrs Dorothy Margaret Tangney who became a Western Australian senator in 1943 for the Labor Party. The first woman member of the House of Representatives was Dame Enid Lyons, the wife of a former prime minister, Joe Lyons. She became the member for Darwin (Tas.) in 1943.

In the 1890s wage levels were so poor that women would walk to and from work to save the fare. Many workers particularly in dressmaking and hatmaking establishments, earned five shillings (50 cents) for a 60-hour working week. These disgraceful conditions were only changed by union influence.

The second woman to return from N.S.W. to England was Dorothy Gray, a dealer convicted of perjury. When she was transported in 1788 she was already 82. In 1793 when she returned still apparently healthy, she was 87.

Equal pay for women in Australia was not granted by the Commonwealth Arbitration Court until 1969, and was not fully introduced until 1972. This followed its partial introduction by the New South Wales Labor Government in 1958.

Words

The early settlers often had to use whatever materials were on hand. The "Wagga blanket" was two layers of cornsacks, between which was stitched a layer of tea-tree bark. A sort of primitive doona.

The word "goanna" for our giant lizard or monitor is a local contraction of "iguana". Early settlers thought that these reptiles were iguanas, which of course, they are not. These days the word goanna is accepted as a totally independent name for the creature, not related to iguana.

It is important to distinguish between a guzinter and a guzunder. A guzinter in old slang is a teacher (two guzinter four) and a guzunder is more recent slang for the bedroom chamber pot (it guzunder the bed).

In the old days a person who was mean and not anxious to spend, was said to have "short arms and long pockets", or to have "death adders in his pockets".

The difference between a "bushman's dinner" and a "bushman's hot dinner", was the mustard.

Some wonderful terms came out of the First World War. An "Anzac button" was a nail used in place of a trouser button. "Anzac soup" was shell-hole water polluted by a corpse, and "Anzac wafers" were hard biscuits supplied in place of bread.

Sunday drivers may bother you with their hazardous driving, but this is nothing new. In the old days the problem was the "Sunday rider", a term used generally for inexperienced horsemen or women.

A "shepherd's lantern" was made by heating a clear bottle near the base until it was hot all the way round, then dipping it in cold water. With a bit of luck the base would crack off cleanly all the way around. Before the neck cooled properly a piece of candle was dropped into it. The neck was therefore used as both a socket to hold the candle and as a handle.

The flogging that the convicts suffered had a terminology all its own. A "red shirt" was a back laid bare by flogging.

WORDS

A "Botany Bay dozen" was 25 lashes. A "bob" was 50, a "bull" was 75 and a "canary" was 100.

Even the early convicts used words with a hint of irony. Their term for the bread they were fed was "scrubbing brushes", because of the effect that the chaff and bran content had on the internal plumbing.

Bundaberg (Qld) is an important centre of the sugar industry. The hessian sugar bag which was used by swagmen and nomadic workers to carry their possessions, was referred to as a "Bundaberg suitcase".

The country around the Darling River is very dry. Old-timers used to refer to the "Darling shower": three claps of thunder, two drops of rain and one dust storm.

If you were asked to sing the "Gawsave" would you know it? It is slang for the national anthem. You know, "Gawsave the Queen".

The word "emu" is not an Aboriginal word—it is a corruption of the Portuguese word "ema" which means ostrich or crane. The Aboriginal word "marriang" would have been a happier choice. "Rosella" is a corruption of "Rosehiller", that is, the bird found at Rosehill (Parramatta, N.S.W.).

A person who was crazy or "cracked" was often described in the old days as being only ninepence halfpenny in the shilling, or said to have "white ants in his billy".

The Australian bushman always had a fine turn of descriptive phrase. One favourite—he was so short that to mount his horse he had to stand on his head to get his foot in the stirrup.

A "slush-lamp" was an unpleasant contraption which was supposed to keep the mosquitoes away as well as provide light. It was a tin of old fat with a rag for a wick. The smoky fumes were enough to stop a buffalo, never mind a mosquito.

When the early settlers started naming the birds and animals they found around them, it would have been simpler if they had stuck with the Aboriginal words. However, they held the Aborigines in such low regard that instead they tried to find some imagined resemblances to a creature that they were familiar with. Some of the names fortunately did not stick. Native bear (koala) and laughing jackass (kookaburra) did not really take on, but other cases such as magpie for the piping shrike, or opossum for something not the same as the American animal, unfortunately gained wide usage.

The term "bobby-dazzler" for something particularly good arose from the name of a famous gold nugget found on the Pilbara goldfield (W.A.) in the 1890s. It weighed over 400 ounces (about 12,400 grams) and would now be worth over $150,000 for its gold content alone. At the time it was valued at £1500.

Farmers are called "cockies" because it was said that the farmer would work hard to clear his land, fence it, plough it and plant wheat in it. The next day he would get up in the morning to find it white with cockatoos grubbing out his seed—a crop of cockatoos or "cockies". Therefore he is a "cocky farmer" or "cocky".

"Dinkum", that most Australian of words meaning genuine or honest, is not an Australian word. It comes from the Lincolnshire dialect in England where it means "fair play".

The oldest Australian riddle, from about 1840.
Q.: "Why is a creditor like a platypus?"
A.: "Because he's a beast with a bill."

A "pommy" is an Englishman. One authority holds that it came about because of their rosy cheeks, red like pomegranates. Another theory is that it grew out of the convict days through use of the letters P.O.M.E. (Prisoner of Mother England) in the convict records.

The word "budgerigar" is an Aboriginal word meaning "good food". That's right, they were a major source of food to the Aborigines.

"Art unions" were originally supposed to be a form of lottery where paintings were offered as prizes for the people who bought shares. Houses, blocks of land, motor cars, T.V. sets, refrigerators and stereograms have been offered as prizes, but seldom paintings.

In the old days a horseman may have put on his dog poisoners (new leggings) and his laughing sides (elastic-sided boots) and gone submarining (riding in long grass). Falling off was described as "riding up a gumtree" or "taking up a selection".

The bangtail muster is an old Australian method of accurately counting cattle on a station, particularly when it is being sold with its stock. The cattle are yarded and put through a crush where the tail tuft is cut off. This prevents them being counted a second time, or driven from place to place on the station to create the impression of greater stock numbers than really exist.

Early this century South Australians were referred to as "croweaters". It has been suggested that this was because of their magpie-shrike emblem which does not look unlike a transfixed crow. Whenever you enter South Australia on the highway, there is a South Australian emblem to welcome you.

An old name for a person from Victoria was "gumsucker", sometimes abbreviated to "sucker". People from New South Wales were "cornstalkers" or "cornstalks", Western Australians were "sandgropers", Queenslanders were "banana benders" and Tasmanians were "apple eaters".

A constant danger to tree fellers were the broken and rotting limbs near the tops of trees. The vibration of the axes and saws, or even a light breeze, could bring them crashing down on their heads. That is why they called such branches "widow makers".

In the early days carrying a broken nose and black eyes was referred to as wearing "the Botany Bay coat of arms".

The old saying—"He's got Buckley's chance" meaning he has no chance at

all, seems to have come from a pun on the name of the old Melbourne department store, Buckley and Nunn. The saying was "he's got two chances— Buckley's and none".

The word "Anzac" was first used in January 1915. A word was required as a telegraphic code to refer to the Australian and New Zealand Army Corps then in France. Cases of supplies stacked and awaiting transport to France showed the initial letters A.N.Z.A.C. At the suggestion of a clerk, Lieutenant A. T. White, the word was created from the initials.

In the early 19th century residents of southern Tasmania were referred to as "barracoutas".

A "wowser" is a kill-joy or a spoil-sport, a person who disapproves of something enjoyable. The word is said to have come from the initials of the phrase: "we only want social evils reformed".

Bush cooks, who cooked for drovers and shearers, were often referred to as "bait-layers". This was a reference to the poisoned baits that were set for dingoes and other pests.

Bushrangers usually required their victims to "bail up". This referred to the practice of cows having their heads held in a "bail" for milking and was the equivalent of an order to stand still.

In the pioneering days food was often far from fresh when it was eaten. This led to food poisoning with accompanying sickness. It was often called the Barcoo rot, Barcoo vomit, or Barcoo spew.

Sometimes the meanings of words are difficult to find. How about a men's lavatory being called a "biscuit factory". Well, it seems that it originated in Adelaide where there was a biscuit manufacturer called Menz.

World Beaters

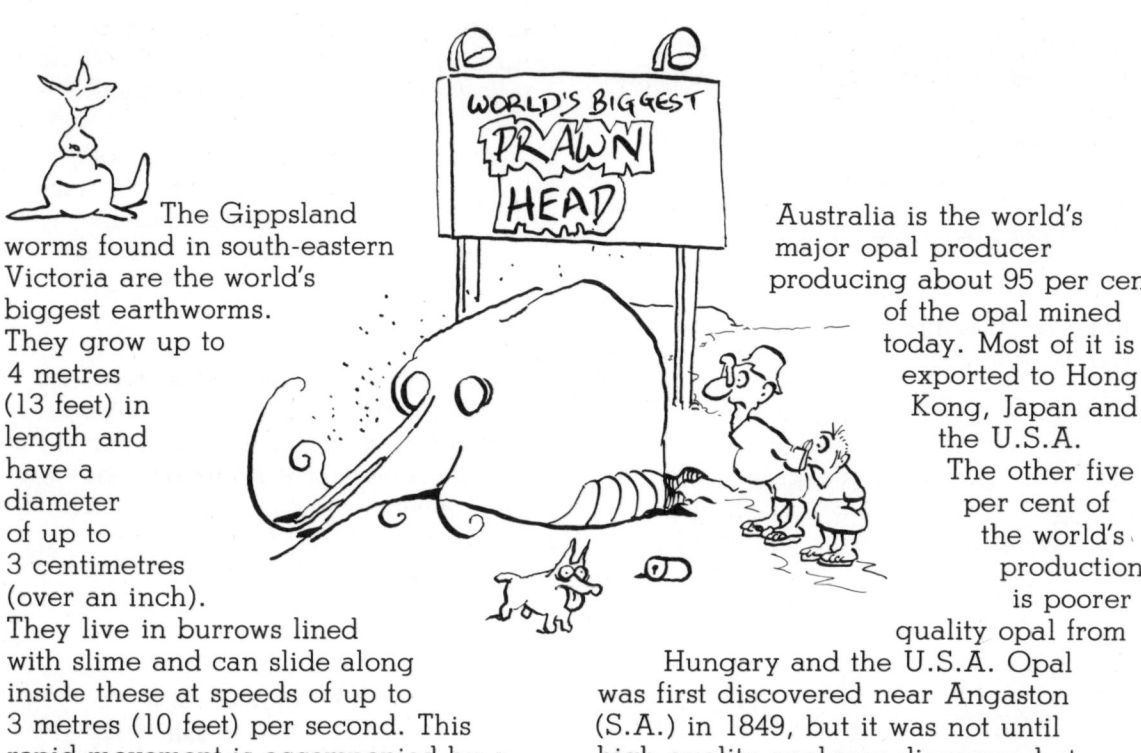

The Gippsland worms found in south-eastern Victoria are the world's biggest earthworms. They grow up to 4 metres (13 feet) in length and have a diameter of up to 3 centimetres (over an inch). They live in burrows lined with slime and can slide along inside these at speeds of up to 3 metres (10 feet) per second. This rapid movement is accompanied by a gurgling sound which can sometimes be heard on the surface.

The oldest ski club in the world is the Kiandra Snow Shoe Club in N.S.W. It was formed in 1870 by miners who strapped slabs of board to their feet and used long poles to keep their balance. They called their homemade skis "snow shoes" or "Kiandra Kick-ins". Despite this early start, Australia has never won a medal at the Winter Olympics.

Australia is the world's largest producer of mineral sand concentrates of rutile, zircon and monazite. We produce over 70 per cent of the world supply.

Australia is the world's major opal producer producing about 95 per cent of the opal mined today. Most of it is exported to Hong Kong, Japan and the U.S.A. The other five per cent of the world's production is poorer quality opal from Hungary and the U.S.A. Opal was first discovered near Angaston (S.A.) in 1849, but it was not until high quality opal was discovered at White Cliffs (N.S.W.) in 1880 that an opal-mining rush started.

Most insects live short, violent lives, but the world's longest-living insects are Australian. Queen termites of the Queensland species *Nasutitermes triodiae* have been proved to live for over 60 years. No wonder they build mounds up to 7 metres (24 feet) high.

The Great Barrier Reef off the coast of Queensland is the largest coral reef in the world. It is about 2000 kilometres (1200 miles) long and up to 72 kilometres (45 miles) wide, with a total area of 210,000 square kilometres. This

WORLD BEATERS

makes it over three times the size of Tasmania.

The world's largest recorded unit of gold-bearing material was dug up at Hill End (N.S.W.) in 1872. This piece of mixed metal and quartz was 1.45 metres (57 inches) high and 38 centimetres (15 inches) wide. It weighed over 200 kilograms (450 pounds). When it was refined it produced over 100 kilograms (3000 ounces) of fine gold. However, it is not counted as a nugget because it was not entirely made of gold.

Fraser Island (or Great Sandy Island) is the biggest sand island in the world. It has an area of over 1554 square kilometres (600 square miles) and contains several freshwater lakes. It is situated across the entrance to Hervey Bay in south-east Queensland.

The world's largest bauxite deposits are at Weipa (Qld) on the coast of the Gulf of Carpentaria. Bauxite, which is the ore used for aluminium production, occurs in highly concentrated deposits which are mined by open-cut methods. It is estimated that there are 3,000,000,000 tons of bauxite at Weipa. Even the cliffs on the beach are made of it.

The world's longest-burning fire is the fire in the coal seam under Mount Wingen (N.S.W.), Australia's "burning mountain". It is estimated to have been burning for thousands of years and there is no indication that it will ever stop. Early visitors to the area thought that there was volcanic action in the area, but it was later found to be a fire.

The world's largest moth is the giant atlas moth *Coscinocera hercules*, found in northern Queensland. It has a wingspan up to 28 centimetres (nearly 12 inches) and was eaten by the Aborigines.

The world's largest crayfish is the Tasmanian crayfish *Astacopsis gouldi*. Found mainly off the coast of Tasmania it can grow up to 50 centimetres in length and weigh over 5 kilograms (13 pounds). Some of the biggest are caught around King Island, which is just as well because there is not much else to do there.

The bulldog ant, found in tropical Queensland, is the world's largest ant, at about 4 centimetres (1½ inches). It is also a very primitive insect thought to have existed largely unchanged for 50 million years.

Australian rice farmers achieve the highest yields per hectare anywhere in the world. The only areas that are more productive are those where three crops a year are grown, but each crop is much poorer than even our poorest crops.

Australia is the world's largest exporter of iron ore. The largest customer is Japan.

The world's largest crystal opal was found at Andamooka (S.A.) in 1969. It weighed 6.16 kilograms (220 ounces) and was valued at $168,000.

The world water speed record is still held by Ken Warby in his turbo-jet hydroplane *Spirit of Australia*. It was set in 1977 on the Blowering Reservoir and is 464 kilometres per hour (290 miles per hour). The engine was taken out of a Sabre jet plane and was prepared by R.A.A.F. technicians from Wagga Wagga (N.S.W.).

The Gladesville Bridge in Sydney is the world's longest concrete arch bridge. It was built in 1964 and is 305 metres (1000 feet) long. Incidentally it was built by a Melbourne contractor.

WORLD BEATERS

The world's biggest glacier is in the Australian Antarctic Territory. It is the Lambert Glacier which is about 500 kilometres (320 miles) long and up to 64 kilometres (50 miles) wide. There are several other giant glaciers in the Australian Antarctic territory.

In an average Australian election about 95 per cent of the eligible voters cast their votes, the world's highest turnout of voters. In the U.S.A. the average turnout is below 60 per cent. One of our favourite pieces of graffiti appeared on a factory wall: "Don't vote, it only encourages them".

Australia has the biggest proportion of naturalised citizens of any country in the world. About one person in 14 has been naturalised after migrating from another country.

The world's largest species of oyster is *Ostrea hyotis* which grows up to 3 kilograms (7 pounds) and is found along the Great Barrier Reef. It is, however, very coarse and unsuitable for eating.

The longest stretch of straight railway line in the world is the part of the standard gauge line which crosses the Nullarbor Plain in South Australia and Western Australia. It runs for 478 kilometres (300 miles) without a bend.

The Nullarbor Plain is the world's largest flat bedrock surface. There are virtually no trees on it, and beneath it are hundreds of unexplored caves.

The 24 metre (80 feet) ferns which grow on Norfolk Island are easily the world's tallest ferns.

The biggest fish ever caught on a rod and line was a white pointer shark weighing 1208 kilograms (2718 pounds). It was caught by Alf Dean at Denial Bay, near Ceduna (S.A.). It was 510 centimetres (about 16 feet) long, and was over 15 times as heavy as Alf.

Most mosses grow close to the ground. Not so the Australian species *Dawsonia superba* which grows 30 centimetres (12 inches high), much higher than any species elsewhere in the world.

WORLD BEATERS

The world's deepest artesian bore is at Blackall (Qld). It is about 2000 metres (6000 feet) deep. Every day about 1600 million litres (about 350 million gallons) of artesian water is discharged from artesian bores in Australia but 90 per cent of that is lost in evaporation and seepage. Eventually the flow is expected to slow up, unless reserves are conserved.

Australia has the world's biggest advertising sign. It is the 183 metre (600 feet) long letters of "Readymix" on the Nullarbor Plain near Bulladonia (W.A.), constructed in December 1971.

The brown coal (lignite) deposits in Victoria's Latrobe Valley are the largest known deposits in the world. In places the main seam is over 70 metres (200 feet) thick. It is so prone to fire in hot weather that in summer it is continuously sprinkled with water, while being mined by open-cut methods.

The "Welcome Stranger" nugget is the largest gold nugget ever found. It was mined in 1869 at Moliagul (Vic.). It weighed 63.95 kilograms (2284 ounces) and was sold for £9584. Nowadays it would be worth over a million dollars.

ANGUS & ROBERTSON PUBLISHERS

Unit 4, Eden Park, 31 Waterloo Road,
North Ryde, NSW, Australia 2113, and
16 Golden Square, London W1R 4BN,
United Kingdom

This book is copyright.
Apart from any fair dealing for the
purposes of private study, research,
criticism or review, as permitted
under the Copyright Act, no part may
be reproduced by any process without
written permission. Inquiries should
be addressed to the publishers.

First published in Australia
by Angus & Robertson Publishers in 1986

Copyright © Stephen Taylor 1986
Illustrations © Patrick Cook 1986

National Library of Australia
Cataloguing-in-publication data
The Australian kids' almanac.
  ISBN 0 207 15090 7.

  1. Australia — Miscellanea — Juvenile literature.
  I. Taylor, Stephen, 1939- , II. Cook,
  Patrick, 1949- .
994'.002

Printed in Australia by the Globe Press Pty Ltd